A Common Privilege

with best wishes

Terry Keene

12/11/96

A COMMON PRIVILEGE

The Story of Outney Common, Bungay

Terry Reeve

MORROW & CO.
BUNGAY, SUFFOLK
1996

First published Morrow & Co, Bungay 1996

ISBN 0 948903 53 8

Designed and typeset by Morrow & Co, Bungay, Suffolk
Printed and bound by St Edmundsbury Press

FOREWORD

THERE was a time when every community, large or small, had its own common land for communal grazing. However, all things change. Some towns have lost their commons and surrounding agricultural land, there are fewer tied cottages, and many towns and cities now have industrial development where sheep and cattle once grazed.

With progress in agriculture, and the increase in leisure activities, those commons which remain are now prized for their landscape value and recreational opportunities. Where stock grazing continues there is the additional benefit of maintaining their nature conservation interest.

Outney Common, Bungay, like the town itself, provides a combination of ancient and modern. There are still the agricultural activities, with the cattle grazing on The Lows during the summer months. This complements the access and leisure activities allowed as a privilege by the Common Owners to the inhabitants of Bungay and others.

Terry Reeve has gone to great lengths to present accurately the history of our Common, and the Common Owners are grateful to have this record for future generations.

W. J. Warnes
Chairman of Bungay Outney Common Owners

Dedication

I have decided to dedicate this book to Megan, our family pet border collie, who is always with me on walks on the Common; and to the living spirit of the Common, which I am certain abides in certain areas of that peaceful sanctuary.

Acknowledgements

IT would not be possible to produce a book like this without the help of many people — those who provided information, loaned or took photographs for use, loaned documents for perusal, or simply helped by chatting about the subject in general, to get the feeling of people about it. My thanks to all of them.

I am particularly grateful to the present Clerk to the Common Owners, Mr. Charles Cunningham, and his wife, Anne, for allowing me into their home on several occasions to scour the minute books for information, drink their coffee and eat their digestive biscuits!

Special thanks are due also to Owners' chairman Mr. John Warnes for agreeing to write the foreword for this book; to my brother, Chris Reeve, for his help in locating information, to Town Recorder Frank Honeywood, and to Peter Morrow for agreeing to publish the work.

Bungay,   *Terry Reeve*
Suffolk
October 1996

Contents

	page
Foreword	(v)
Outney Reverie	1
Introduction	3
1. The Origins	5
2. Early Controversies	11
3. Commoners & Common Reeves	23
4. Rules — Breach & Enforcement	31
5. Waveney's Famed Navigation	45
6. The Coming of the Railway	49
7. Sport & Recreation	52
8. Sir Alfred Munnings	73
9. The Dr. Beard Case & the 1st World War	76
10. The 1920s — Pumped Water & the Suffolk Show	88
11. The 1930s — More Controversies	96
12. Fire!	105
13. Common Registration — Who Owns Outney?	111
14. Protests & Battle Lines	123
15. The Decision — & the People's Privilege	130
16. Flora & Fauna	140
17. Common Bits & Pieces	151
18. George's Epitaph	167
Appendix I	169
Appendix II	176
Appendix III	180
Bibliography	181

Illustrations

page

1. Early flint items found on the Common   7
2. The oldest known Common document, 1665   15
3. 1707 document, signed by 56 " owners"   20
4. *Outney Common* by Thomas Bardwell, 1738   26
5. Map of Outney Common, 1772   27
6. Notice ofthe annual Town Meeting, 1811   32

Colour Plates (between pages 38 - 39)

     1707 document, with seals
     Stained glass memorial to Sir H. Rider Haggard
     Aerial view of Outney Common
     Bungay Races by Sir Alfred Munnings

7. Common (fen) Reeves public notice, 1865   41
8. A map of the Common   43
9. The original golf club house, 1894   58
10. Presentations at the golf club house, c1900   59
11. The Common, from Bath Hills, c1905   60
12. Golf on the Common in the 1920s   61
13. Poster for Bungay Races, April 1920   64
14. Bungay boys watching the races, 1920s   65
15. Race day crowds at Bungay Races, 1909   66
16. The race card for a Bungay race meeting, 1885   67
17. The scene at Bungay Races , c1909   68
18. The fashions at Bungay races, 1906   69
19. Taking the waterjump at Bungay Races, 1904   70
20. Coming home to win, Whitsun meeting of 1909   71

21. George Baldry and his wife, 1947 — 84
22. The picturesque Bath House, 1900s — 85
23. Boating on the Waveney — 86
24. The Mill House — 87
25. Finches Well, 1915 — 91
26. Cricket teams, c1895, bricklayers v carpenters — 92
27. The Bungay Carnival Band, c1925 — 93
28. Water pumping station, 1924 — 94
29. Train, Bungay Station — 100
30. Common Bailiff, Broomy Baldry — 101
31. Demonstration, January, 1976 — 124
32. March and rally in January, 1976 — 125
33. Silver Jubilee plaque, 1977 — 145
34. The unchanging scene on The Lows — 146
35. Dusk on Outney Common — 148
36. The bridge over the former railway line — 149
37. Edwardian scene, fishing and boating — 153
38. Finches Well — 154
39. Blackberry bushes on Outney Common — 165
40. Flora and fauna — 166

OUTNEY REVERIE

The old town stands behind me now — and there ahead
Lies Outney Common and the evening sky;
A nature's paradise and land of dreams,
Exquisite now as Bath Hills dons her gown
Of sunset red, and cradles Waven's stream.

The summer scents of sun on yellow gorse and fern
Have given way to fragrances of even':
Of misty mellowness of marshes where
The sweet aromas of the buttercup and thyme
And willowherb enfold the senses there.

There is a place down close to Waven's edge from
where,
Framed by a window in the trees I glimpse
The distant stature of St Mary's spire
Which, caught by brush strokes of an evening sun,
Presents a picture of a greater fire.

The skylark still his soaring song relates, and yet
It merges with the silence of the scene,
And with the linnet, finch and Jenny wren,
Its notes embrace the beauty, fill the air
Of this fair corner of a Suffolk fen.

O Nature, turn to music to compose this scene,
And make our Waveney land a gentle chord;
A symphony for flute and harp amend.
An Outney reverie to pastoral peace,
That stills the flow of the most gifted pen.
And now you're there, mid silent silhouettes of scattered
oaks,

Knee deep amidst the softness of the grass.
Your smile as always gentle on your face;
And in this time and in this pleasant place
I wish this moment now should never pass.

In this quiet spot where twilight shadows subtly merge
With rustic boughs, wild rose and blackberry,
You're surely there among the nature things.
The birds, the weeping willow, flowers — and you
Are my companions in the hush that even' brings.

We stroll and talk by Waven's lilied stream, and share
The closeness of our thoughts and of the scene,
In this Common — and yet far from common — land;
Alone, together, in what's now become
The garden paradise of this man's heaven.

At last towards the towered town I turn again;
But lingers yet the warmth and memories
To savour long — till next I 'scape to roam
And dream amongst the fragrances beneath
A Bungay sky, in Outney fields of home.

BUNGAY, JULY 10TH, 1989

2

INTRODUCTION

THE Common — to most people it is known simply as that. Even pet dogs respond knowingly and eagerly to those two words.

The Common — Outney Common, Bungay — covers 390 acres (it used to be over 400 before the railway was built) of heathland and grazing marshes to the north of the town, contained within a great loop of the River Waveney, and sheltered to the north by the beautiful Bath Hills, protecting Bungay and protected by it.

The higher ground is known as The Hards, and the pasture as The Lows, names that have endured for centuries. It is owned by the Outney Common Owners, who run it and take the profits, after expenses, in dividends. From ancient times it has been divided into portions known as goings, or commages, each comprising a little over an acre. A going is still the term used for each owner's share. Some own several of them.

The townspeople use the Common for recreation, and always have. It has been a favourite place for walks ever since "promenades" became fashionable in the early part of the 18th century. Then, people walked across the Common to take a medicinal cold bath at Mr John King's establishment, served by a spring at what were then known as The Vineyard Hills. John Barber Scott records walks there in his 19th century diaries: " April 27th, Sunday, 1828 — in the evening we walk on the Common and Bath Hills. Nightingales sing boldly." Today more people than ever walk in those picturesque surroundings and use it to exercise their dogs.

Many people have fond memories of the Common — their first romantic meeting, their hole-in-one on the golf course, escapades while boating on the river, the inevitable " big fish" stories of anglers, swimming at Sandy, Finch's Well or Toby's Hole, picnics, family fun, making camps in the gorse, getting lost, snowball fights, cheeking the bailiff.

3

A Common Privilege

The Common has always played a significant part in Bungay life in many ways, as its back garden or working venue. It is a fascinating place for the botanist and naturalist, reflecting the seasons in the rich yellow of the gorse in early summer, the purple splashes of willowherb later, the myriad of colours in the grasses in the autumn, the beauty of its winter snowscapes.

It has been described at various times as " the most interesting Common in East Anglia," its race course " the most picturesque in England except for Doncaster," one of its plants, a blackberry, is found in greater abundance there than anywhere in Britain, and it helped to inspire one great artist to paint.

The hope is that this book will inspire many people's fond memories of times they have had there (though it does not set out to record them) as it traces its history over the centuries — a history that has been as colourful, in a different way, and certainly controversial.

It is chequered with disputes and arguments, mainly between the townspeople and those who have run the Common — confrontations prompted on the one hand by the fact that Bungay people have always felt they have a right to use the Common as common land, and on the other by efforts, and the perceived need, for it to be run on a sound management basis.

The basic working use of the Common has changed little for more than 1000 years — the grazing of cattle for food and for a living. Today that primary use still survives alongside its role as Bungay's largest and most enduring recreational amenity.

This is Outney Common — The Common; a land for all seasons.

Chapter 1
The Origins

On Outney Common there are plenty of traces
of historic man, as well as some earthworks which
have been assigned to various periods. In July,
1904, I spent several days in rambling about the
Common, and soon discovered that my searches
for Neolithic relics was likely to be best rewarded
by confining my attention to two or three
grassless hollows...projecting into the marshy
part of the Common (The Lows)...

Archæologist William Dutt, writing in 1905.

How old is Bungay Common? How was it formed? The answer to the first question can be only approximate, but very roughly it is 470,000-500,000 years old. As to the second question, it happened something like this.

Around half a million years ago, as the remaining ice sheets left by the Great Ice Age that swept down from the north gradually melted, the geography of East Anglia as we know it today took shape.

Before that, the River Thames flowed north-east over much of what is now Suffolk. The final phase of the Ice Age, the Anglian glaciation, wiped that out, the Thames diverted to its present valley to the south, and new river valleys were formed. They were revealed as the waters from the melting ice left deposits of boulder clay and gravel.

One of these was the River Waveney — its general east-west line was established at that time. More detailed features evolved over the thousands of years that followed, sculptured by further cold periods (called periglacial and interglacial periods), by erosion, thawing, changing sea levels, and subsidence.

As with most of the rest of East Anglia, the area would have been inhabited by such wild animals as huge elephants, lions, hyæna and bison. The recent discovery of a fossilised elephant at Cromer in North Norfolk is firm evidence of that — it is thought to have weighed eight or nine tonnes and stood 13ft high at the shoulder, a huge animal compared to modern standards. The vertebræ of a similar elephant has been found at Ditchingham in the past, and the foreleg of a bison was discovered at Earsham Gravel Pits in 1989.

At this time Britain was still joined to mainland Europe. It was not until 6000-7000 years ago that the North Sea made Britain an island, and as seas receded, rivers shrank in width, leaving wider and wider flood plains. Features we can recognise today gradually took shape — among them the 400 green acres we now know as Bungay Common.

Eight thousand years ago it would have been a bare landscape. Later a coniferous forest would have been established there, and by 5000BC mixed oak trees would have been the main feature.

A palæolithic axe-head found on the Common in 1989 is evidence that man had visited the area by this time, but it was probably about 5000 years ago, in the Neolithic period, that it first saw more established settlers. Neolithic man would have put up primitive huts along the line of the river, on the high ground on the Common and the area now occupied by Bungay itself.

Archaeologist William Dutt, in a booklet *The Waveney Valley in the Stone Age,* written in 1905, claims firm evidence of Neolithic man on the Common. The fascinating book tells how his searches proved highly productive on two low hillocks situated on The Lows.

" Here I found a beautifully made leaf-shaped arrow head, and a javelin head which had unfortunately lost its point; also some scrapers, and two flakes which had evidently been used as a saw," he wrote.

Several " curious depressions" in the vicinity, some almost circular, he felt bore a close resemblance to hut circles, though he conceded that they could have been caused simply by recent digging for sand.

1. A Paleolithic hand-axe found on Outney Common by Matthew Davey of Bungay in 1989. It is 150, 000 years old.

2. Plano-convex knife of the late Neolithic or early Bronze Age.

3. Flint knives of neolithic or early Bronze Age, similar to those found on Outney Common by William Dutt.

4. Neolithic flint knife or blade, circa 4000 BC, similar to the one found on Outney Common by the author.

5. Neolithic axe-head, 3500-2000 BC.
(Bungay Museum Collection)

Dutt also records finding an excellent example of a Neolithic polished axe, 5.75 inches long and 2.25 inches wide, made of grey flint. He also found a triangular knife, and in another area of the Common, human bones which he was convinced belonged to prehistoric inhabitants. Flint flakes were numerous, he said, and he found several scrapers.

Sadly, what became of the items Dutt collected is not known. But when I decided to test his theories recently (1990) on the two hillocks on The Lows, in just 15 minutes I picked up a number of flints and flakes, one of which was positively identified as a Neolithic fabricator — the sort of tool that would have been used for such tasks as skinning animals, and perhaps cutting meat.

So Neolithic man does seem to have been the first to have carved out an existence in any permanent way — the first farmers perhaps — on what we now know as The Common, working on the high ground beside the then wide waters of the Waveney. Hunting animals, growing crops, clearing woodland and rearing animals would have been their annual round. They probably kept cattle, pigs, sheep and goats — and so that very earliest use of the Common is one still in use today 5000 years later, as cattle feed on the grazing marshes.

In those early days, of course, they were simply occupiers of free land, not owners of portions of land known as " goings" , a system which will be explained later.

In this Neolithic period it is easy to imagine what the scene might have been like beside the Waveney — men clad in skins, probably with long hair and beards, skinning animals, cooking on fires outside their wooden huts, animals grazing over a wide area, fishing going on in the river and flint implements being " knapped," eyes always alert to any danger, with the line of hills we know as Bath Hills providing the backdrop to the scene.

The Neolithic Age evolved into the Bronze Age and that in turn into the Iron Age, but the Common seems to have been less well populated in these periods, and there have been no " finds" relating to them there. Bronze and iron would have been hard to come by in this part of the country.

For this reason it may have been that in these periods flint implements continued to be used here, or people moved to areas where new tools were developed. Modern day feelings that new developments reach East Anglia later than most areas perhaps follows an age old trend!

The vegetation of the Common would have changed over this pre-historic period through climate, usage by wild animals and primitive man cutting down trees for huts and warmth. The Waveney would have been wider, filling its flood plain, leaving The Hards, the higher ground, the only area above water, though the river would have been tidal. Indeed, even up to the Roman period the Waveney at Bungay would have been estuarine — that is, it would have started to form its estuary, opening into the North Sea, at a much closer point to Bungay, than it does today.

As the centuries moved on into the period AD, Queen Boudicca and her Iceni tribe, and then the invading Romans, who conquered her Norfolk and Suffolk strongholds, may well have made use of the Common for various purposes. Stone Street, built by the Romans, ran between Halesworth and Tasburgh via Wainford Bridge on the outskirts of Bungay, and there is thought to have been a military fort at Wainford until AD70.

A Roman coin was found on the edge of the Common and was dated AD62. Now the latest evidence of finds at Wainford suggests that the Roman establishment there was much more significant than previously thought. If that was the case, it may be that Roman soldiers were the first to use the Common as a military training area. In any event the word Common comes from the Latin communia and developed the meaning of a piece of unenclosed land, or " waste," belonging to a local community.

In Roman times there were probably other such areas of communia in the Bungay area. This one, probably during the Saxon period, came to be known as Outney Common.

The origin of the name Outney undoubtedly has to do with its position, which at the time was very marshy at best, and under water for long periods at worst. The suffix -ey means landing place or quay, or from the Saxon means " island or dry land in marsh." Both would fit Outney very well.

It is similar to Stepney, which was " Stybba's Landing Place," or Hackney, " Hakka's Landing Place." In Outney's case the Outn part must have been someone's name — Outa, or Otta, perhaps, but there is no clue to this, even in the Domesday book. However, Adrian Room's book on British place names suggests that Ouse, as in the River Ouse, means water, as in the French *eau*, and also relates to 'otter' and 'wet'.

Chapter 2
Early Controversies

Anyone who observes the position of Bungay with regard to the river would perceive that it was by nature a very strong military position, and in ancient times when the river was surrounded by impassable marshes, there could be no access whatever to the dry ground, except from the south.

B. B. Woodward.
19th century Bungay historian

With the Romans having departed these shores, local people were left in comparative peace to go about their business of living and survival. But the Romans had left the legacy of demonstrating that geographically the area around the Waveney Valley was a good one for permanent settlement, and primitive military thinking told inhabitants that the high ground fronting the Common, with the Waveney protecting it, was a good one defensively.

In those early times, as Woodward said, the impassable marshes surrounding the river would have meant the only access to the settlement was from the south. Even earlier settlers, probably the Celts, had dug a defensive ditch across the " neck" of the Common as added protection. Part of that ditch, sometimes referred to as the pullery ditch, was still visible within living memory — it passed through what is now Clays' factory, but the last visible signs of it disappeared with the building of the Bungay bypass in 1983.

The vantage point on which Bungay now stands was thus almost an island, with the land encircled by it and the loop of the Waveney becoming The Common — vacant, but from the very earliest times valuable for grazing and a source of many material assets.

It was a family of Angles who set up home on the headland as, in the four centuries leading up to the Norman Conquest of 1066, the present pattern of villages and towns in Suffolk was established. It was probably originally known as Le Bon Eye — The Good Island because of its unique position, a name which eventually evolved into Bungay. In the Domesday Book its Latin name is Bongeia.

At the time of the Norman Conquest the Common would have been well used by inhabitants. At that time, Godric owned Bungay Burgh and Stigand owned Bungay Soke.The Common is not mentioned by name in the Domesday Book which William I commissioned soon after his victory at Hastings, but there is no doubt that its 400 or so acres were among those included in the survey of Bungay. Districts called Hundreds had already been established by then, and Bungay and the Common were in Wainford Hundred. Ten manors are mentioned in the Domesday Book Bungay entries, and a total of about 534 acres, plus a number of carucates (areas of ploughed land), and areas of woodland. Bungay's population then was about 250-300.

So names mentioned in Domesday would have been among those who " held" the Common before the Norman Conquest, or afterwards in the King's name — such men as Stigand, Godric, Wulfmer, Alwin, Alfger, Aelfric, Ulfketel, and Summerled. Howard and Edric were others. All would have made good use of the Common in ensuing years . When Roger Bigod built Bungay Castle in the 12th century he may well have used materials from the Common — wood, perhaps gravel, reeds and furze, and flint.

Later when Hugh Bigod was in dispute with Henry II, it was partly the protection afforded his castle by the marshy Common, and the Waveney, which led him to declare: " Were I in my castle at Bungay, upon the River Waveney, I would not fear the King of Cockney."

Later still another Roger Bigod, grandson of Hugh, is said to have flooded all the lowland meadows around the castle, including the Common, in defiance of Henry III, presumably to double the protection.

Meadows were valued highly and protected carefully. Like the arable land, they were often allocated by lot and shared out afresh each year, and it is conceivable that the system of goings on Outney Common had its early origins from that time, and evolved from that.

The lords of the manor — at Bungay, the Bigods and their successor Dukes of Norfolk — would have had their own strips in the system.

From medieval times onwards, many pieces of common land such as these were encroached on or enclosed. Open fields, greens, commons and marshland were taken as enclosures by landowners, yeomen and peasant farmers through the Middle Ages and up to the 17th century. Sometimes this was done by the command of the landowners, sometimes by agreement, sometimes by registration with a legal court, and sometimes (probably less often) by a Parliamentary Act. By this means people appropriated land and fenced it in for their own individual ownership.

But this does not appear to have happened with Outney Common. It may well be that there was a system of allotted strips of land on it, but people pastured their stock there and continued to enjoy common rights.

There is no written evidence of how the system of goings on Outney Common evolved — but that it did evolve from the manorial system, from Bigods' time or before, is highly likely. Successive members of the Bigod family held the title of Dukes of Norfolk and Suffolk. The last of these, Roger Bigod, who rebuilt and crenellated Bungay castle in 1294, made Edward I heir to all his castles, manors and possessions, including the castle and lands at Bungay. In due course Edward II gave all the possessions of the late Roger Bigod to his own half-brother, Thomas Plantagenet, whose surname was de Brotherton, and who was created Earl of Norfolk.

They were valued at the time at 6000 marks, and the land gifted almost certainly included the Common.

By the time Lord Howard, a succeeding Duke of Norfolk, was slain at the Battle of Bosworth in 1485, the family is said to have had no more use for the castle, but the land continued as part of the manor, and the inhabitants rights to graze their animals on it continued.

At some stage, perhaps even before this time — there is no written evidence to say exactly when — what we know today as goings, or shares in the Common, became attached to properties in the town, mainly in the parish of St Mary's. The right to graze cattle on a going became, in effect, part of that property, and would have been a valuable asset at that time. No deeds exist to say how a going, or goings, became attached to properties, but in later times there is ample evidence of them being sold away from properties.

It would be appropriate at this stage to introduce the Bungay Town Trust and the office of Town Reeve of Bungay. The popular theory in Bungay is that the title of Town Reeve, who heads the Town Trust, goes back to Anglo-Saxon times. It is not until the first half of the 16th century that there is mention of a Town Reeve by name — then William Brooke appears in the St Mary's churchwardens' book of 1536, suggesting that the title had been established sometime before then.

The Town Trust became the administrative body of the town, with the Town Reeve and members of the Trust, called feoffees, also administering town lands.

The first deed in existence relating to town lands is dated May 6th, 1639, conveying land at Bungay and the parishes of Earsham, Hempnall and Ilketshall to 24 of the most honest, discreet and sufficient inhabitants to manage in trust, and to spend the income belonging to the town of Bungay. These 24 individuals were the Town Trust feoffees.

The land conveyed in that deed, known as a feoffment, included " all that piece of meadow with free ingress and regress to and from Outney Common in Bungay aforesaid." It is the only mention of Outney Common in the deed, but it does add, after listing specific areas of land, " all other lands, etc., lying within the town of Bungay."

These items are recorded in the Town Trust minute books. There is nothing to say that the Town Trust or Town Reeve had any direct responsibility for the letting of goings on the Common or for its management, but their close links with the Common Reeves, or Fen Reeves, who looked after the Common, are detailed later.

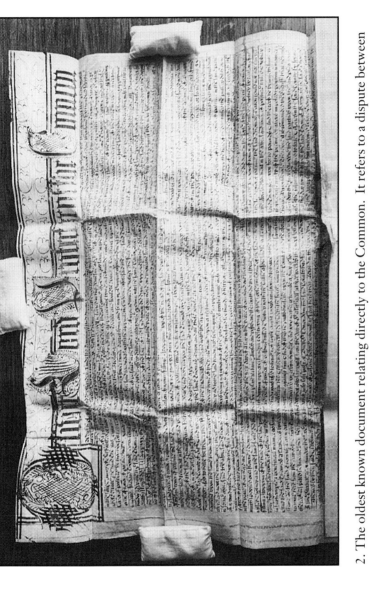

2. The oldest known document relating directly to the Common. It refers to a dispute between Thomas Matthews and Thomas Bacon, relating to the stopping up of the pullery ditch linking the river across the 'neck' of the Common, causing flooding, dated 1655. (*Suffolk Records Office*).

To return to the matter of goings being attached to properties in Bungay, one of those who had such a property may well have been Thomas Bacon, who featured in a court case in the middle of the 17th century, recorded in a four-page document dated January 7th, 1651.

It refers to the stopping up illegally of the pullery ditch, across the " neck" of the Common. It was a dispute explained more fully four years later in a document dated Westminster, November 28th, 1655, the record of a court case in which Thomas Bacon, a gentleman, accused Thomas Matthews, a miller, of causing flooding there by blocking the ditch.

Thomas Bacon had, " tyme out of mind, had the right of pasturage for two horses and a foule Levant and Couchant on a certain piece of pasture called Outney Common."

But Thomas Matthews, " being ignorant of the premises, did on the first day of January in the yere of our Lord 1651 at Bungay, with earth and stones, fill and stop up the pullery dytch or water course opening into the same Common river called Waveney, and running through the same piece of Common and pasture called Outney, and in the August following the same piece of common and pasture was much spoiled and overflowne and drowned with water, and also on the first day of May in the year of our Lord 1652 at Bungay aforesaid did on the soil of the said piece of common and pasture then and there enclose half an acre of the said piece of common pasture. For his trespass, Thom. Bacon claimed forty pounds."

Matthews was found guilty and Bacon was awarded £7 damages and £14 10s costs and charges by the court.

The pullery ditch is frequently mentioned in the Duke of Norfolk's 1688 survey of Bungay in identifying the location of houses and messuages. Outney Common is also frequently mentioned, though not in terms of use of goings on it, or the attachment of goings to properties.

A typical entry in the survey is: " Elizabetha, wife of Richard Gooday...holds the freehold of a one messuage house...situated between the tenement of John Belward to the south and William Dunston and Gillingwater to the north, and abutting the road leading to Outney Common called Broad Street to the west, and the road leading to Outney Common called Nether Way, or Back Lane (today's Nethergate Street) to the east."

For the legal purposes of the time, matters appertaining to the Common came under the jurisdiction of the manor courts, and there are many references to this in the Court Books kept at the Duke of Norfolk's Arundel Castle archives. From them it is clear that it was not necessarily the poor people of the town who abused the Common, or grazed cattle there when they were not entitled to do so.

The Court Book for the period 1670-1692 (archive M381) contains several enlightening entries. Thomas Walcot, for instance, a wealthy Bungay gentleman who owned navigation rights on the River Waveney at Bungay, was before the court on May 20th, 1678, for digging out turf from the Common when he had no authority. Osmund Clarke, who held the court, fined him 6d " and it is ordered that he should not do the same again under pain of 20s."

At the same court Robert Harvey was said to have " overburdened the Common belonging to this manor with bullocks, as he should not by right," and was fined 1s, with the same 20s to pay should he do it again — something like the suspended sentence of today.

On May 23rd, 1670 Robert Taylor, Edmund Twaights, Robert Cooper, Robert Nursey, John Belward, Isaac Smith and Robert Jenkerson (the last three known from records to be men of substance in Bungay) were all fined for " overburdening the Common called Outney, contrary to the ancient custom of the town." Owen Harvey was dealt with because he " unjustly commoned" there.

When William Downing and John Cleere were each fined 12d on June 12th, 1671, for unjustly commoning, they were given 11 days to remove their cattle.

The court sitting on May 15th, 1676, outlined " the ancient custom of and concerning the Common called Outney Common to be that no person shall common on the same at any time thenceforward more than one great beast, whether ox, horse, cow or foal." It is a significant declaration, which will be explored further later, and includes no mention of owners.

Officials of the manor put forward information on alleged offenders to the court, which continued to deal from time to time with people who broke the rules on the Common — rules which obviously went back a long way. On May 28th, 1683, for instance, Robert Cushing overburdened the Common by pasturing three milk cows there, and was fined 5s (the phrase was " therefore he is in mercy 5s.").

And in 1687 John Jones jun., really seems to have gone over the top. The court on May 16th that year, before Joshua Nelson, the steward, heard he overburdened the Common " by pasturing on the same diverse great numbers of pigs, which according to the customs of the common pasture aforesaid are not commonable cattle. Therefore he is in mercy 10s. And it is ordered that he shall not do the same or anything of a similar nature after May 20th, 1687, under pain of £5..."

A steep suspended penalty indeed for those times!

These court records are ample evidence of the problems of management of the Common, on which many people depended for their survival. Quite simply the Common was being overgrazed — and probably always had been.

The pasture had no respite throughout the year, and grazing it in the winter was wearing it down and giving it little chance of recovering properly in the spring. The result was that cattle were not fattening, calving or milking as they should, and that affected prices for them at the market — and probably the quality of butter and cheese as well.

There had been grumbling among those using the Common about this for some years, particularly against those mainly responsible for putting their animals on the Common, both the Hards and The Lows, at all times of the year.

There was talk of the need to have a period when there was no grazing at all, to allow the grass time to recover, and to further limit the number of animals allowed to graze at any one time. It appears the limit per going had been five for as long as anyone could remember.

The matter came to a head at a meeting on January 20th, 1707. The issue was debated at length by a large number of Common users, and at the end of their discussions, in which the Duke of Norfolk's representative had an input, they decided to reduce the number of beasts per going from five to three, in an effort to preserve the pasture — a significant change in those days when so many depended on the animals for their foods.

The document which embodied this change refers to the " ancient custom" of Common usage, making it clear that the rights it referred to went back a very long way even at that time. It refers to the users as commoners, and there is no mention in it of fen reeves, Common Reeves or anyone else managing the Common.

The wording on the 1707 document says: " Ancient custom or manner of commoning upon the common pasture called Outney in Bungay, belonging to the manors of Bungay Soke and Bungay Burgh, hath been or hath bin reputed to be that every person having a right of commonage or food upon the said common pasture, have fod for food and depasture thereupon five beasts only, that is to say five milk cows, five working horses, being either a horse or a colt, upon his messuage or tenement or lands by which he hath right of commonage with the apurtances Levant and Couchant every year as to his said messuage or tenement or lands..."

Significantly, the 56 people who signed the document, with seals, were headed by Edmund Bacon and the Duke of Norfolk's appointed steward for the two manors involved, Joshua Nelson. Many of the other signatories, such as John Dalling, Gregory Clarke, Richard Nelson, Philip Girling, John King and Samuel Hemblin (bailiff of the manors), were leading citizens of Bungay at the time,

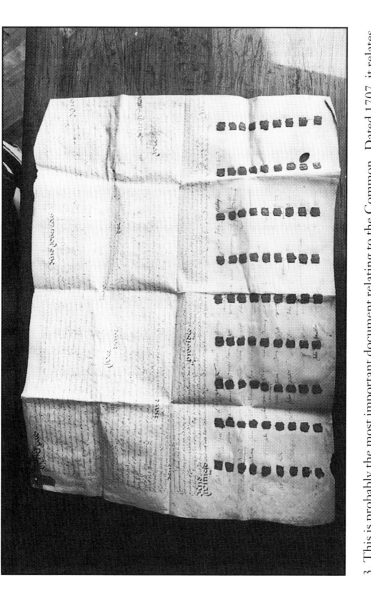

3. This is probably the most important document relating to the Common. Dated 1707, it relates to the management of it, and is signed by 56 people who were, effectively, the first Owners. (*Suffolk Records Office*).

many were undoubtedly members of the Town Trust, and some would have served as Town Reeve.

Not only did they agree to a reduction in the number of beasts per going — they went further still in their determined attempt to establish good management of the pasture. The document referred to people putting their beasts on the Common throughout the year " without having any regard to the winter season, or the springing of the growth of the grass...so that the summer season affords but little food or benefit to them and the rest of the commoners.

If the Common was spared and not fod for some reasonable time in or towards the spring of the year, all the said commoners would reap greater benefit and advantage thereby."

Therefore, said the announcement: " No one at all shall keep any cattle or beasts whatever on the Common between the first day of February and the 20th day of April in any year hereafter for ever." This was to be done so the Common would be " spared up for the preserving of the growth and better improvement of the food there for the benefit of the said commoners."

With some variations in the dates, that rule has held firm to the present day. The number of commonages varied from time to time, but some years later became fixed at 150, with 300 goings, the figure which is the same today.

The 1707 document is a key one in the history of the Common, and is evidence that the feoffees of the Town Trust had a strong influence over what happened there. That was further confirmed in a Town Trust deed of 1719.

This directed that the feoffees should present their annual accounts at a meeting on the first Tuesday in December each year, and also laid down guidelines for the election of the Town Reeve. From that date, fen reeves to manage the Common were elected at the same meeting, when their accounts were also presented.

It may well be that between 1707 and 1719 it became apparent that Fen Reeves were needed to manage the Common, taking on that role from the manor bailiff. His role in the town would have covered many other duties. But this may also signal the time when the Common became separated from the Duke of Norfolk's holdings.

The Fen Reeves records date from this time and from 1719 they kept separate records of the December meeting. In the Fen Reeves' book the annual accounts are signed by the Fen Reeves and the inhabitants of the town, with the name of the Town Reeve invariably being at the top of the list of signatories.

Just a few months after the 1719 deed was signed, the Fen Reeves' accounts of May 4th, 1720, showed there were 145 commonages paid for, and 386 beasts on them. This was still too many, it seems, because soon after the number of beasts per going was reduced from three to two, with a cow and suckling calf counting as one.

Chapter 3
Commoners & Common Reeves

Beethoven composed nine symphonies in his lifetime. In one day, between dawn and dusk, the skylark composes hundreds.

QED, BBC1, March 14th, 1990.

(The skylark is the commonest bird to be found on Outney Common).

The documents and records that have been outlined so far enable a clear picture to be built up of how the management of Outney Common developed between 1650 and 1720. It is clear, for instance, that a two-tier system of use of the Common grazing had been operating long before this period. The court records show that the ancient custom in Bungay was that all inhabitants had the right to " common" one great beast there, while other particular inhabitants had, also by " ancient custom," according to the 1707 document, extra rights of commonage attached to the specific properties they owned, whether buildings or land.

These rights allowed them to graze up to five animals on the Common until the changes made in 1707, though the case involving Thomas Bacon seems to indicate that not everyone used these rights to capacity. The 1655 report says Bacon had, " tyme out of mind," the right to pasture two horses and a foule (foal) there, and while it is possible that at that time the number of animals allowed varied according to different properties, it is much more likely that he did not use his right to graze the five allowed to the full.

Those with the rights attached to their properties were men of substance and influence in Bungay, and it was they who got together to convene the meeting to sort out what was happening on the

Common — the poor people allowed just one animal would have had little or no say in it, though it is evident from the court records that the property and landowners were just as guilty as the poor people, if not more so, of over-grazing the pasture.

It is clear, too, that the Duke of Norfolk was party to the decisions made at the meeting on January 20th, 1707, through his steward and his bailiff, who were there. He was the Lord of the Manor. As has been said already, it is not known when, or precisely how, the extra rights became attached to property in Bungay, but they must have been granted by the Lord of the Manor, in return for money or services rendered.

The difficulty in controlling the number of animals on the Common had increased over a number of years and sorting the problems out was a losing battle for the bailiff. The meeting sought the views of property owners on what was to be done, and resulted in them taking on more responsibility themselves, in conjunction with the Town Trust, and with the appointment of Fen Reeves which quickly followed.

The measures agreed on meant more work in carrying them out and trying to see the regulations were adhered to, and there was inevitably a cost involved. The Fen Reeves' accounts of 1720 show that rent was paid for the use of goings to graze animals, with the money going to those who held the rights and used to meet expenses.

Those holding them were still referred to as commoners — but it is fair to say that those 56 people who signed the 1707 document effectively became the first Common Owners and it also marked the watershed at which, had he not decided to do so previously, the Duke of Norfolk relinquished his hold on the Common, to all intents and purposes.

The Town Trust's involvement in the new arrangements is clear from the documents. It may be that the town lands had goings attached to them before that time, but the Trust certainly held one not long afterwards.

Its accounts for 1731 show that the Trust received a rent of 5s for one going. But it is right to emphasise that the ancient custom of all inhabitants to graze one animal continued at this time.

The Reeves' (from now on they will be referred to as Common Reeves) account books which survive date from 1746, and show that in that year the 300 goings were held by 85 people. The Reeves elected at that December meeting were William Kingsbury, John Wicks, Richard Nelson (who served as Town Reeve several times) and Charles Cocking. The usual custom was for each one to serve for two years, although they often served again at a later date.

Those 1746 accounts show that income from the Common that year was £22 5s 2½d, representing a profit of £5 4s 6½d, money which was simply carried forward to the next year. Income included £2 9s paid in fines by trespasses — that is, animals allowed to be on the Common by their owners when they did not have the right to be there. It also included proceeds from the sale of a wide ranging number of commodities which were the Common's natural resources.

These items were all available, and undoubtedly used, in the days before the radical changes to the Common set up in the period around the turn of the 17th and 18th centuries. What is not clear is whether they were previously taken free, as part of the individual's common right, or whether payment was made to the Lord of the Manor.

The accounts give a good insight into what was involved in the running of a Common of Outney's size — it was certainly one of the largest in Suffolk. It was not simply a matter of checking whose cows went on and off and at what time, that booking fees were paid for them and rent paid for the goings. It is easy to imagine the busy scene in Broad Street, Nethergate Street, and the Drift at Outney Road at the beginning and end of each day as cattle were herded by their owners to and fro for milking, but "depasturing beasts" was by no means the only commercial enterprise carried out by the Owners.

4. Probably the most famous sketch of Outney Common, dated 1738 and drawn by Thomas Bardwell. It is a view looking across the Common from the town, with Bath Hills in the left background. Note the double gallows in the foreground, and the bridge across the river, the remains of which can still be seen.

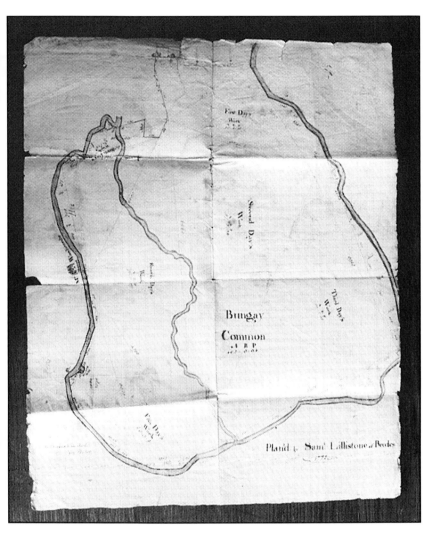

5. A map of Outney Common, dated 1772, by Samuel Lillestone of Beccles. It clearly shows the route of the old river through the Lows, and is a map of the week's work, perhaps for those cutting thistles and nettles, or a mole catcher. *(Suffolk Records Office)*.

Anything on the Common that was a saleable commodity was sold, to gain income and help cover the many expenses that cropped up. Rushes for thatching and flooring, turf for firing, furze, stone, gravel, flag (stones), silt and shingle were all saleable items mentioned in those early accounts, and all had to be monitored by the reeves and those they employed to help them — there were always those ready to take advantage of a situation if they were not vigilant.

Expenses were many. As has been said, the marshy Lows frequently flooded in winter, and it was not uncommon for the bridges over the Old River (which in those days dissected The Lows and still fills today after heavy rain) or the dykes, or indeed the main Waveney, to be damaged or swept away. One item in 1768 is for paying three men " to get the bridges out of the flood," and the sequel appeared the following year — buying 1500 bricks to build a replacement bridge, suggesting that one was a bridge over the main or Old River.

Animals often got stuck in the mud or dykes and had to be pulled out — payments were regularly made to men for this work: " 1755 — to James Mapes, drawing two beasts out of the mire, 1s," is just one example. And the men that did the work had to be sustained, with the cost of beer for refreshment often appearing in the records. Reed cutting was another expense — it was entered as " cutting the river."

Yet another job was " cutting down the thistles and nettles all over the Common" — an item that was a costly 13s 4d in 1763. Then there were the moles, just as much a nuisance in those days as they are today. Catching them was a skilled job which the Owners were happy to pay for. The going rate in the mid-18th century was 1d a mole and in one year the catcher did particularly well, with 148 caught.

In many cases the reeves used the Town Crier to advertise the particular jobs that needed doing, and to let people know that it was time to book goings for the season — a system of booking them had quickly been established following the decisions of the early part of the century. A typical entry in the accounts was, in 1762: " For crying notices for all persons to book their goings, 1s."

Those "keeping the Drift" — establishing the ownership of cattle going on and off the Common, and probably also keeping an eye open for animals which had not been booked on — also had to be paid. Horse stealing was rife at that time throughout the country, and was a crime punishable by hanging.

The cattle plague that raced through Britain in the middle of the 18th century did not leave the Common and those who used it untouched. East Anglia was badly affected, and the Common Reeves' accounts of 1747 include payment " to Will Evans for watching the horned cattle for certificates, 5s." As part of the effort to control the plague, inspectors issued certificates to those owners whose cattle were unaffected. The Bungay Gentlemen's Club made collections for those affected, with one entry in its' records reading:

" December 26th, 1748. Collected at the club for John Bracey at the Bath House, for his loss of five cows and calves, ten shillings and sixpence." They may have represented all he owned, though whether they grazed on the Common is not known.

It has already been said that the commonages were originally attached to properties, and it was only later that they began to be sold separately from them. Many instances occur in various archives of the sale of properties with commonages. One random example from the Norwich Mercury in the 1740s reads:

" Bungay — house for sale in the Market Place. Three rooms on a floor, two large cellars and storehouse, stable and outhouse. Right of commonage for four beasts on Bungay Common..." There is no doubt that they would have been a useful selling point.

The Common had been a depository for those who died in the Black Death in the 14th century. There were many victims in Bungay and the bodies were simply put into one large grave, which came to be known as the plague pit. It is now covered by the 17th green of the golf course which lies, in fact, on the floor of a large pit on the Common just in front of the water pumping station.

Some 400 years later, when the scourge of smallpox hit this country, it was the Common again which was used to take the sufferers. A pest house was built there in about 1730, sited on what is now the fairway for the second hole of the golf course, in the dip beyond the first rise when travelling north from the club house. Until the course was altered some years ago the old 17th green was more or less on the pest house site with the green, oddly, called the Plague Pit hole. From the air, the outline of the pesthouse foundations — it was a fairly small building — can just be seen.

It was built at the expense of the Town Trust, and was well used. Its isolated spot away from the town was to try to contain the disease, but vigilance was needed, and people were paid " for watching the smallpox house" to try to prevent those there making their way back into town.

Smallpox claimed the lives of many Bungay people. Eventually, the Shipmeadow workhouse was built three miles away, and patients were sent there. Bungay's pesthouse was no longer needed, and it was sold in 1770 for £40, to Miles Abrow, with the proceeds going to the Town Trust.

What with the smallpox and the cattle plague, the Common was not the most inviting place in the middle of the 18th century!

Chapter 4
Rules — Breach & Enforcement

The Common's wide plain that to Bungay belongs,
Was crowded with beauty's and loyalty's throngs;
Where a bullock, whole-roasted, ten gallons of beer,
With full two thousand loaves did the populace cheer.
Here a scene of vast splendour saluted the eye,
From the flower-spangled turf and the sun-beamy sky...

From a poem written on the celebration of the
coronation of King George IV, July 19th, 1821.

The running of the Common, keeping an eye on its resources, getting the best deals from them and organising the use of the goings in a proper way was a business on its own, run largely by the Common Reeves appointed at the annual town meeting.

Finally, towards the end of the 18th century, comes the first written mention of the commoners as proprietors, though the document involved again links them very closely with the Town Trust. It seems that the commoners and the Town Trust bought the newly erected Ditchingham Mill, and the Mill House, in a complicated arrangement because they were worried about the effect a mill would have on the Common. It stood just on the Norfolk side of the Waveney, beside the public footpath from the Common.

The Common Reeves' accounts records that the mill was bought in 1784 from Thomas Woodward and William Browne, with the document of sale signed by 45 commoners, and was said to be for the benefit of the Common. The Town Trust minute book records that the then Town Reeve, Thomas Manning, bought Ditchingham Mill in 1784 for £200 from Mr Dixon Gamble, a feoffee who was Town Reeve himself two years later. The minutes say the mill was

BUNGAY
Annual Town Meeting
DECEMBER 3rd. 1811.

ORDERED that the DRIFTAGE of BUNGAY COMMON for the present year be *four shillings* for each head of Stock, and that the said Driftage be paid at the time of Booking. the Goings, to Mr. W. DYBALL, Bookeeper.

And further that *sixpence* be paid for every load of Gravel by every person not an Owner; and that Owners pay *fourpence* per load for the same.

Ordered that in future every ASS belonging to a poor person, be allowed to be depastured on BUNGAY COMMON for *five shillings*, and every ASS belonging to a Tradesman, shall in future pay *twenty shillings* for the same, to be left to the discretion of the *Fen Reeves*.

6. The public notice announcing the annual town Meeting of 1811.

taken on the Town Reeve's account and mortgaged to Mr Manning " because its new erection was injurious to Bungay Common."

There was, at the very least, close financial co-operation between the two bodies, and the situation is made clearer in a document of 1811, a year after the Town Reeve and feoffees had agreed, on December 4th, 1810, to sell the Mill House and its land to pay off land taxes. It was sold to Captain Samuel Sutton and his wife, Charlotte, of Ditchingham Lodge, and the sale document, dated October 11th, 1811, says it was originally bought in 1784 " in trust for the benefit of the township of Bungay, and to the extent that the said trustees or feoffees, their heirs and successors, should be debarred from building, erecting, raising or making any mill sluice, dam, weir or other such like work upon the said premises or any part thereof, and in trust for the owners and proprietors of commonages and common rights of depasturing beasts upon the common pasture of Outney in Bungay aforesaid. And whereas the said Thomas Manning, Inigo van Kamp, Poll, Burstall, Plowman and Gamble are all dead, leaving the said John Cooper then surviving, and whereas at a general town meeting of the proprietors of commonages on the said Common, and other inhabitants of the said town, for the managing and ordering of the affairs of the said township immemorially held on the first Tuesday in the month of December in every year, and accordingly held on Tuesday, the 4th of December last past, it was ordered and determined that the cottage, land and heriditaments hereinafter mentioned should be sold by public auction at the King's Head Inn in Bungay aforesaid on the 28th day of February last past, subject to the condition and agreement hereinafter mentioned."

It is an interesting deed which clearly indicates that the Common Owners — as they will be called from now on — and the inhabitants jointly " managed and ordered" Bungay's affairs. This joint annual meeting of Owners and Town Trust which started in 1719 continued until well into the second half of the 19th century. It should be bourne in mind that many feoffees of the Town Trust, if not all, would have been Common Owners also.

Captain and Mrs Sutton paid £250 for the Mill House (sometimes referred to as the mill cottage).

Mrs Sutton was in fact the daughter of the Rev. John Ives, who had been the subject of a rebuke by the Common Owners at the meeting of December 1st, 1795. It demonstrated they showed no favours to rich or poor when it came to controlling the Common, and it showed, too, that those at all levels of society would take advantage of the Common's resources if they could.

On this occasion the Rev. Ives, who lived in Bridge Street, and who apparently had a reputation of being able to "drink any man under the table," was severely criticised. The account in the Common Reeves' book says:

It being the opinion of the meeting that great damage has been done to the Common by the very large quantity of gravel which has been carted thence by the order of the Rev. Mr. Ives: resolved that in future Mr Ives be permitted to cart the screening of the Great Gravel Pit only, and that his workmen shall not be suffered to remove any gravel whatsoever from any part of the said Common, nor any other than screenings from the Great Gravel Pit.

We can only assume that the Rev. Ives (who that same year befriended the Frenchman Francois Chateaubriand after he arrived penniless in Suffolk and then was injured in a fall from a horse) accepted the decision, which was made to protect the Common. The Town Trust record of the December 1st, 1795, meeting, incidentally, mentions receipt of rent from the letting of goings which it held.

Yet another instance of the dovetailing of the Common Owners and Town Trust comes in the accounts of the meeting of December 3rd, 1811 — it is clear that W. Dyball kept both lots of accounts, for he signed the Town Trust minutes as Town Clerk and the Common Reeves account as book-keeper. The two books recorded different matters, however, with the Common Reeves' account showing that that year Outney Common driftage was fixed at 4s for each head of stock, to be paid at the time of booking the goings, with the price of a load of gravel fixed at 6d for those who were not Common Owners and 4d for Owners.

The meeting also took steps to help the poor; "Ordered that in future every ass belonging to a poor person be allowed to be depastured on Bungay Common for five shillings, and every ass belonging to a tradesman shall in future pay 20s for the same, to be left to the discretion of the Common Reeves." A good number of the poor people took advantage of the offer, and were no doubt grateful for it.

The interweaving of the Owners and Trust continued until well into the second half of the 19th century. But though they worked closely they were clearly separate, with separate finances, as illustrated in a loan made by the Town Trust to the Common Reeves in 1807. It can be argued, of course, that the Town Trust would only agree to such an arrangement with a body with which it was closely linked, and which it recognised as a legally constituted body.

The record of the transaction is included in the Town Trust minutes of the town meeting of December 6th, 1807:

We whose names are herewith subscribed, being Common Reeves properly appointed, do hereby acknowledge to have received of John Cooper Esq., as Town Reeve, the sum of £130 for the use of the said Common, which we promise and agree to pay to the Town Reeve for the time being as soon as possible by yearly instalments.

This loan arrangement was signed by Common Reeves Sam Simonds, Thomas Reason, R. Frith, Plowman and W. Denny. Two years later the reeves were loaned a further £70 by the Town Reeve "for the use of the said Common." The following year the Town Reeve and feoffees agreed to charge 4 per cent interest on the loan, which had all been repaid by December, 1813, at a meeting at which the Common Owners took far reaching steps to counteract abuse of the Common system by its users which had been going on for a number of years.

The loan arrangement needed by the Common Reeves clearly suggests they had got into debt in the running of it, and that does raise one intriguing thought: being in debt, why did they not seek a loan from the Common Owners, most of whom were men of substance, rather than the Town Trust? It would have been the more logical and straightforward thing to do.

The answer may lie with John Cooper, Town Reeve 14 times, and at the time of the transaction one of the few surviving Town Trust feoffees. By 1809 he was the only one, and apparently appointed 42 others himself. It is quite possible all were Common Owners.

Periodically throughout most of the 18th and 19th centuries, there were occasions when the Owners made determined attempts to get the management of Outney Common on to a firmer footing. Things would go well for a while, but abuse of its assets continued, and brought conflict between the Owners, users and Bungay inhabitants to a head from time to time. The 1813 meeting was a good instance of this.

Clearly, in carrying out their role of enforcing the regulations on the Common, the Common Reeves suffered considerable abuse and sometimes threats from those who used it, and mis-used it. Whether mis-use was through ignorance or negligence, or was deliberate, is not clear, but there were certainly people who resented the fact that the use of common land, which they felt belonged to the town of Bungay, was controlled by a body of people calling themselves Owners.

In the 20th century people felt that Outney Common had been the people's Common from "time immemorial," and that view would have been even more apparent through the 18th and 19th centuries. So in the early 19th century people were making a stand.

Certainly that is the feeling to be gathered from the general town meeting of December 7th, 1813, when discussions and resolutions represented a clear attempt by the Common Owners to stamp out any challenge to their authority. This was the outcome of that meeting:

At a general town meeting of the Owners of commonages on Bungay Common and the inhabitants of Bungay on the 7th of December, 1813, the following resolutions for preventing depredations on the said Common, and the better regulation thereof, were agreed to:

1. All beasts found thereon, not being booked, will positively be adjudged trespassers and fined accordingly.

2. That Owners as well as others shall book all such goings as they may occupy, whether in their own right or otherwise, the same as if hired of any other person, or be adjudged or fined as trespassers; and in future the book-keeper will deliver to each person a printed voucher at the time of entry.

3. For every transfer made after the first booking, the book-keeper is authorised to demand of the hirer, or person making the transfer, one shilling, and no going shall be transferred for less than 14 days from the date of such transfer.

4. It having been a frequent practise with many people that have had goings unoccupied at the time of driving to claim and make a profit by taking from the drift such cattle as would have proved trespassers, thereby doing great injury to the rightful occupiers and defrauding the funds of the said Common, the fen reeves for the time being are empowered the more effectually to prevent such impositions in the future, to detain all such cattle as they may think proper, 'till they are satisfied of the justices of the claim made for the same, whether by persons in their own right or by transfer.

5. As frequent disturbances have been experienced by the fen reeves, to their great annoyance, in the execution of their duty, by disorderly and ill-disposed persons, and many depredations committed in consequence thereof, all persons offending in the like manner after this notice will be prosecuted and made an example of, at the entire expense of the funds arising from the driftage of the said Common.

6. That the regulations of December, 1807, for detaining stock not claimed and taken from the drift on the day of driving, be adhered to.

7. In future no part of the funds arising from the driftage of the Common are to be expended for any purposes whatever without the concurrence of all the fen reeves, or at least a majority of them.

8. That all cattle not reclaimed from the drift on or before the hour of eight o'clock in the evening of the said driving of the

Common should be detained by the fen reeves as trespassers in any place they may appoint; and all reasonable expenses for keeping and detaining the said cattle from the above time should be discharged by the Owners of the cattle so detained under the regulation.

M. Kerrison Esq., W. Plowman, Esq., R. Butcher Esq., R. Smith Esq., Fen Reeves.

It was strong stuff. Basically, it appears that owners of cattle on the Common (who in many cases were also Common Owners) were in the habit of " pulling a fast one" by using cattle, impounded as trespassers, as their own, saying they had been on goings that were, in fact, unoccupied, or certainly not booked. In this way the Common Reeves were denied income from fines the trespassers would normally have been liable to pay. No doubt deals were done between those involved in avoiding these fines.

The report suggests that some owners of cattle got quite nasty when confronted by the fen reeves about this defrauding, and the whole aim of the new regulations was by way of a " get tough" policy. In the ensuing few years there were no further reports on the issue, so perhaps the steps proved effective.

It was, at any rate, an effort to bring some order to a matter which had become a serious problem, and to show that the Common Owners were keen to demonstrate their authority. But even at this time, there is no record of any chairman of the Common Owners, or even any senior reeve who presided at their meetings. We are left to assume that meetings other than the annual meeting (though there seem to have been few) were called by the fen reeves if any of them felt there were matters that needed discussing.

At the meeting on December 4th, 1821, branding of animals is mentioned for the first time, as the Owners continued to allow poor people to graze their asses on the Common for 5s, " such asses being first branded upon the shoulder according to the direction of the fen reeves for the time being." Tradesmen's asses were also to be branded. At this time 14 people took advantage of the facility, and 17 the following year. In 1822, overall income from the

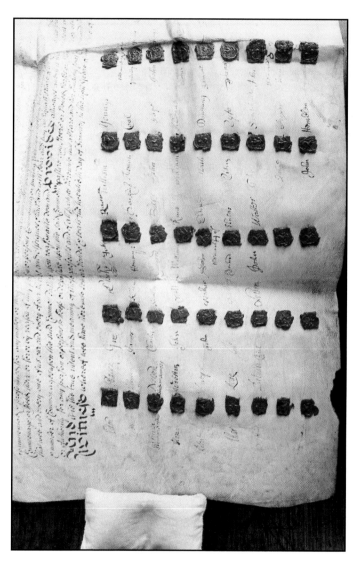

The signatures, with seals, on the 1707 document relating to the management of Outney Common (*Suffolk Records Office*).

A painting of a scene at the races on Bungay Common by artist Alfred Munnings, who came to be known as one of the greatest painters of horses. It clearly shows his signature in the bottom left hand corner. (© *Hunterian Art Gallery, Glasgow University*).

A section of the stained glass window at St Mary's Church, Ditchingham, installed as a memorial to the author Sir Henry Rider Haggard by his daughter, Lilias. It depicts his favourite view across the Common to Bungay.

An aerial view of Outney Common, showing the golf course, its bunkers and the network of footpaths and tracks on The Hards. The Lows grazing meadows are to the right. The road in the foreground takes the line of the former Waveney Valley railway.

Common was £89 11s 6d, with a working balance on the year of £1 13s 7d. Two years later, mowing thistles on the Common cost £2 10s.

The financial records of the Common Reeves were well kept. They included ledgers, drift books with lists of owners, tenants and occupiers, as well as details of donkey goings, bank account books, and gravel and flag account books covering the sale of stones, gravel, silt, shingle and turf. They provided a good insight into the day to day working of the Common. As a random example, in 1852 there were 60 Common Owners, among them the Town Estate feoffees. The executors of the late Inigo Spilling held the most goings, 17. Furze cost 17s a load, screened gravel 1s a load, unscreened gravel 6d, silt 3d and turf 2s 6d for 100ft.

But despite the care, and the backing of the regulations drawn up in 1813, there were still people ready to abuse the facilities and take advantage of them if they could, and a notice issued on February 26th, 1846, said:

Bungay Common — £2 reward. Depredations having been committed on Bungay Common by cutting the rails of the new stock bridge, cutting down a rubbing post and carrying away the same, a reward of £2 will be given to any person who will give such information as will bring the offender or offenders to justice.

And notice is also hereby given that any person found stealing manure, or taking gravel, furze or flag from off the said Common without a note from Mr John Taylor will be prosecuted as the law directs.

John Taylor was the person responsible for the sale of items from the Common and seeing that charges for them were received. He may have been the first clerk to the Common Owners, though W. Dyball effectively filled that role some years before as book-keeper. But George Baker was the first named Clerk. His name appears on another notice issued in 1865 as people continued to ignore the rules and regulations to take advantage of the Common's considerable material assets. Dated January 2nd, 1865, it read:

Bungay Common — whereas depredations have on various occasions been committed on the said Common by persons illegally gathering and removing dung, lighting fires, cutting and taking away furze, carting gravel, silt and soil, cutting turf, damaging posts, rails, gates, bridges, water trucks, drains and doing other unlawful acts thereon:

The fen reeves hereby give notice that any person or persons detected after this day committing any of the above offences will be prosecuted according to the law.

And they further give notice that all stock found upon Bungay Common after Monday, the 15th inst. not duly booked, will be considered trespassers and will be dealt with as such.

By order of the Fen Reeves. Signed George Baker, Clerk.

The fact that a series of notices of this sort were issued over the years is an indication that people continued to ignore the rules and regulations. It is not known whether anyone was prosecuted under the rules laid down, though damage to property, which seemed to happen regularly, was certainly an offence under the laws of the time. Whether anyone could make charges of taking away dung, silt, gravel or furze from the Common stick is not so certain. There are no records of any definitive bylaws governing these things, and the right, or not, of the people of Bungay to make use of materials was at best vague.

Clearly the Common Owners and the Common Reeves realised this and significant changes took place later the same year in another conscious effort to put the Outney Common management on a much sounder footing.

It brought the first appearance of the Outney Common minute book, as opposed to the Common Reeves' accounts book, and the appointment of a chairman — certainly the first Owners' chairman on record — Joseph Parrington.

He told the Owners meeting at the Fleece Hotel on December 19th, 1865 (it is worth noting that it was not the first Tuesday in the month) that the Volunteer Corps had requested the use of the Common for drill and rifle practice, but that recently " persons had

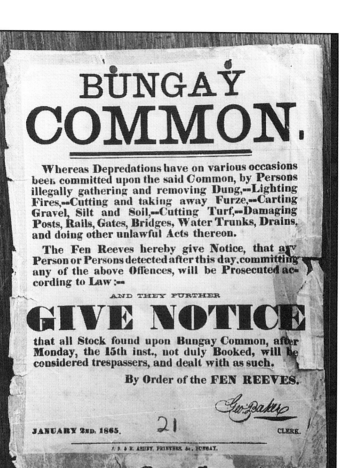

BUNGAY
COMMON.

Whereas Depredations have on various occasions been committed upon the said Common, by Persons illegally gathering and removing Dung,—Lighting Fires,—Cutting and taking away Furze,—Carting Gravel, Silt and Soil,—Cutting Turf,—Damaging Posts, Rails, Gates, Bridges, Water Trunks, Drains, and doing other unlawful Acts thereon.

The Fen Reeves hereby give Notice, that any Person or Persons detected after this day, committing any of the above Offences, will be Prosecuted according to Law :—

AND THEY FURTHER

GIVE NOTICE

that all Stock found upon Bungay Common, after Monday, the 15th inst., not duly Booked, will be considered trespassers, and dealt with as such.

By Order of the FEN REEVES.

Geo. Baker

JANUARY 2ND. 1865.   21   CLERK.

J. B. & E. ASHBY, PRINTERS &c., BUNGAY.

7. A typical public notice issued by the Common (fen) Reeves in their efforts to control abuse of the Common and its material assets. This one is dated January 2nd, 1865, and signed by clerk George Baker.

presumed to erect barriers on the Common and to demand payment for admission to the enclosure made."

Large quantities of turf had been removed for the purposes of making a cricket ground "and all these acts have been committed without any leave of licence from the Common Reeves."

The meeting heard a letter of apology from the cricket club secretary, Dr James Gardiner. He said he had been told by one of the reeves, Mr Smith, of St Mary's Street, that there would be no objection to taking turf, but on no account would an enclosure be allowed. In a second letter he said the lack of an application was "quite unintentional, and from ignorance of the laws and regulations." It was left to the Common Reeves to decide if the cricket ground should be allowed to be completed and more turf taken.

The episode illustrates that it was certainly normal practice at the time for Bungay people to ask the Owners or the Reeves for permission to do things on the Common.

Common Reeves elected at that meeting were Mr Parrington, Mr Samuel Smith, Mr John Rackham, Mr Robert Dyball, Mr Henry Smith and Mr Robert Playford, and for the next 17 years they and the Common Owners strove to achieve their desire for "better regulation" of the Common. The opportunity arose to re-affirm their legal basis following the passing of the 1878 Enclosure Act, which supplemented one of the same title passed in 1845.

A meeting of the Owners on March 28th, 1883, at the Odd Fellows Hall, agreed to take steps to obtain a provisional order for the regulation of Outney Common under the provisions of the two Acts. Solicitors were instructed, and in the meantime the Owners appointed an agent for the first time. He was Henry Rushmer, given a salary of £15 a year, with a role which also included that of clerk, and the power to employ a bailiff at not more than 14s a year.

Rushmer's brief was to manage the affairs of the Common, with full powers to regulate the times of turning on of stock (the Hards being open all year), the sale of materials and the prices for them.

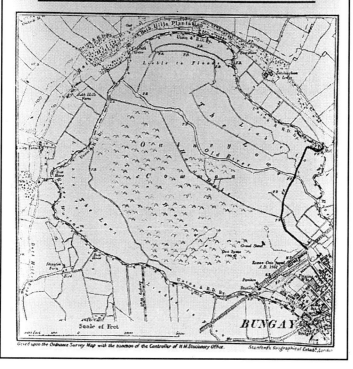

8. A map of the Common, kept in Bungay Museum, showing the
public footpath running over The Lows to Ditchingham. It is still
the only official footpath over the Common. The map also shows
the site of the former pest house.

An Outney Common account was opened at Gurney's Bank (now Barclay's) in the town .

Eight months later, at a meeting on January 4th, 1884, solicitors advised that there would need to be a two-thirds majority in value of the Common Owners to assent in writing to the application for a provisional order under the Act. At that stage 35 Owners (with 170 goings) had agreed and there were 18 (130 goings) from whom assent was not obtained — so the two-thirds necessary was not achieved. (Main owners at the time were William Hartcup, with 34, Sir Edward Kerrison, with 28, and Samuel Scott with 26).

However, solicitors advised that if the Common went back to the old system of management (not outlined in the minutes) " such a system could not be legally enforced. A return to it therefore would in all probability cause the property to deteriorate in value, and would only result in the postponement of the final settlement to a future day. In our opinion it is very desirable to have the management of the Common placed on a sound and permanent footing."

They made the position abundantly clear. But the Owners at the meeting (16 of them) concluded that " as it appears impossible at the present time to obtain a provisional order for the regulation of the Common," Rushmer's appointment should be confirmed. They went on to appoint William Hartcup, John Rackham, H. W. Owles and Lewis Bull as Common Reeves for the year.

The inference was that this was a meeting vital to the future of the Common and that an opportunity to put it on a sound management footing for the first time had been lost.

Chapter 5
Waveney's Famed Navigation

You've heard of old Bungay — her fam'd navigation
Her Waveney, the pride and delight of her Town;
That brings to her wharf the choice wares of the nation;
And adds every year to her wealth and renown.
You've heard too of Diss, and her duck-pond of
puddle;
Her Mere, fam'd for mud, and of reptiles the den;
You've heard of Diss beer, which we drink — and not
fuddle'
Of her ginger-bread cakes and her Diss-honest men!
And now you shall hear how these Diss-honest fellows,
Have a project to make us all wonder and stare:
'Tis to steal all the trade from Old Bungay — they tell
us -
By joining Diss pond to the Waveney and Yare.

From S. Ashby's *New Navigation*, 1820.

No book on Outney Common would be complete without recording the highly controversial plan of 1818 to extend navigation on the River Waveney from Bungay to Diss. It may not have affected the Common directly, but the result of digging a cut across Bungay to cut out the large loop of the river around it could have dramatically affected the drainage of The Lows, that part of the river and thus the physical geography of the area.

Navigation from Yarmouth to Bungay had been opened in 1672, and since then the town had survived on a healthy commercial trade, with wherries bringing a wide range of commodities, including coal, timber and grain, to The Staithe from Yarmouth. The trade had made Matthias Kerrison, who owned the navigation rights at the time, a millionaire.

But in 1818 a group of Yarmouth businessmen saw the opportunity of further wealth if the river was opened up even beyond Bungay, to Diss.

Their idea was to deepen the river, cleanse it, straighten out many of the meanders and, at Bungay, build a cut, removing the loop around Outney Common from the main route.

It seems this cut would have left the main river somewhere near the Wainford Lock and rejoined it near Flixton, perhaps crossing Beccles Road in the Mile End area, and going through now built-up areas of the town. Alternatively, it could have taken a route where the present bypass is. Had that happened, where would the railway have been built 42 years later? In any event it would have meant major alteration to the geography of the town, and Bungay may well have developed in a completely different way.

Those matters did not trouble Bungay businessmen and civic heads at the time — but they were very firmly against the scheme. After a meeting at the New Hall at Yarmouth on January 19th, 1818, had resolved that the promoters of the scheme should apply for an Act of Parliament to further it, the Town Reeve of Bungay, John Scott, called a public meeting at the Three Tuns Hotel to debate Bungay's response.

It was held on February 5th and 200 people attended. They heard that the plan was to form a stock company to raise the necessary funds for the far reaching project, which would have involved eight miles of new cuts in all, widening, straightening and cleaning 12 miles of the river, and building 11 new locks and 25 bridges. The estimated cost of £37,931 was a vast sum for those days.

Opening the river navigation to Diss would benefit 46,000 inhabitants over a wide area on either side of the Waveney Valley, including those at Diss, Eye, Harleston and Halesworth, it was said.

But the meeting dismissed the idea as "a ruse by Yarmouth to draw trade from places such as Diss and Eye." It was said that the owners of the present navigation rights to Bungay, Mr Kerrison, and mill owners, even though they would benefit, were against it. The

Rev. Chester was particularly outspoken at the meeting. He said it would "introduce a system of plunder and depredation hitherto unknown."

The meeting unanimously agreed that the plan "would be highly injurious to the lands, rights and comforts of individuals." It agreed to give "all lawful opposition to the project." Norfolk and Suffolk MPs were urged to oppose the plans in Parliament, and the meeting agreed that Bungay should petition the Government on the issue.

A committee — today it would be called an action group, no doubt — was formed under the chairmanship of Mr. J. J. Bedingfield to plan a local campaign, and part of this was a petition signed by many inhabitants and leading businessmen of the town. The view of the Common Owners on the issue is not recorded, but undoubtedly they would have been among those signing the petition.

Mr. Ashby's verse also included these lines:

> *Old Bungay arouse thee, maintain thy proud station -*
> *With thy hills and thy castle, thy Waveney and town;*
> *Bid thy sons guard their rights in the old navigation,*
> *Which adds every year to thy wealth and renown.*

That is what Bungay did. Meanwhile a meeting at Diss, seeing that it could benefit from navigation up to its doorstep in the same way that Bungay had, supported the idea. But Thetford opposed it.

The Yarmouth petition calling for an Act to approve the plan was duly presented to the House of Commons on February 13th that year. Bungay's reaction was to publish a notice asking for subscriptions for a fighting fund.

In the event, Yarmouth withdrew its proposal, and the Bungay petition against it was never presented to Parliament. Businessmen, inhabitants and Common Owners alike breathed a sigh of relief.

Another attempt was made in 1865 with a similar project. This time a Bill was put before Parliament for the "widening, deepening and diverting of the stream of the River Waveney and purchasing navigation rights, mills and other properties thereon between Lopham, Lowestoft and Yarmouth."

This time the Common Owners did discuss it, at their meeting on December 19th at The Fleece. Their minutes record that they felt the scheme would be "injurious to the interests of the Common Owners," and unanimously agreed to oppose it.

Once again, the scheme came to nothing, and Waveney's great loop around Outney Common remains uncompromised to this day.

Chapter 6
The Coming of the Railway

Whether covered with winter snow, carpeted with bluebells in spring, heady with the scent of tufted grass and gorse in high summer, or offering up its fruits in autumn, Outney Common is a place well used always, by farmers, sportsmen, ramblers, children, families, lovers...a land for all seasons, Bungay's biggest and more enduring asset.

The railway revolution which transformed transport in Britain in the middle of the 19th century reached Bungay in the early 1860s — and brought with it a fundamental change to the geography of Outney Common. The " iron road" dissected it, leaving, in effect, two commons — the main Common and the other, a narrow strip on the town side of the railway line, which quickly came to be known as the Little Common, or Small Common.

Until that time, the Common began roughly where the gates are at the top of Outney Road which now leads to Clay's lorry park; and at the Broad Street gate which was situated about 50 yards on the town side of the present bypass roundabout.

Book printers' Clay's had not arrived at Bungay at that time, and there was an area on the edge of the Common known as the Hop Ground — hop growing was a major industry in Bungay during the 17th and 18th centuries. The Eastern Counties Railway Company brought the railway from Harleston to Bungay in 1860 — it was opened on November 2nd that year, and a move was soon made to extend it through Bungay to Beccles.

For this purpose the company bought the Hop Ground in 1861 for £420 — an area of about five and a half acres in all. The Common owners were the vendors, and it was they who concluded the agreement for the sale.

The line to Beccles, linking Bungay to the East Suffolk network, was opened on March 1st, 1863, and at that time the Eastern Counties company was amalgamated with the Great Eastern Railway. The following year, on July 28th, 1864, an agreement was signed between the Owners and the GER, under the provisions of the Land Clauses Consolidation Act of 1845, to extinguish the rights of common over the land which was then part of the railway system.

On November 11th the same year a deed poll compensating the Owners for loss of those common rights was signed — the second of two documents which were to play a significant part in deciding the future of the Common over 100 years later.

From that time, access to the Common was via a level crossing at the Broad Street entrance, and a brick bridge at the Outney Road end. The landscape there changed rapidly over the years as railway buildings, sidings, fences, telegraph poles, a signal box and passenger buildings went up, with regular negotiations taking place between the Owners and the railway company (who also acquired the land on which the coalyard and sidings were sited), the gas company (on the matter of laying pipes across the Little Common to light the station) in 1867, and the Postmaster General (to allow telegraph lines to be erected to the station at a charge of 1s a year) in 1869.

These various utilities found the Common Owners sometimes difficult to negotiate with. In April, 1886, for example, they could not reach agreement with the GER for a siding on the Little Common for the loading of cattle. And on January 19th, 1909, the Owners told the GER that the rent of £10 a year for leased land at the station was inadequate and should be doubled to £20. If the company did not accept the increase it was to be given notice to quit! That would have produced an interesting situation. But at their next meeting the Owners heard the company had agreed to the rise.

The railway was of course something of an attraction, particularly for children, who delighted in leaning over the bridge to watch the trains go under, and then dashing to the other side as it came out again. The fact that it covered their faces with smuts of soot did not bother them at all. Watching the engines take on water at the water tower up line from the bridge was another attraction of a visit to the Common — the railway, its trains, carriages, goods wagons and general activities had instantly become part of the Common scene, and remained so for almost exactly 100 years.

Passenger services finally ended on the Waveney Valley line in January, 1953, 90 years after they had begun, and goods services ended about 10 years later. All traces in Bungay of the magnificent age of steam engines finally disappeared when the Bungay road bypass was built along the route of the line and opened in 1983. The brick bridge to the Common was replaced by a footbridge, but the heavy lorries and juggernauts that use the road today have never been such an attraction for children as the old steam engines were.

Chapter 7
Sport & Recreation

On summer evenings, when the shadows are long and the grass is high, when the cattle are statues in the grazing meadows, and the sun still warm and drawing out the fragrances from marsh and gorse, when swifts and swallows chase playfully beneath the blue sky and the river drifts, sultry slow, through the peacefulness: this is my favourite Outney time, when the stillness is undisturbed, and you can dream your dreams and walk closely with God.

For centuries the primary role of Outney Common was as a place where inhabitants of Bungay could graze their animals, and as a source of materials to make their existence easier — necessities of life such as wood, furze, gravel and so on. It was not until the last century that it really began to come into its own as a place of recreation, sport and leisure.

True, the children of Neolithic man probably played the games that Neolithic children played while their parents hunted and cooked. The Romans encamped at Wainford could well have had more organised "games" on the land; and in medieval times and the days of the Bigods, who built Bungay Castle, it is conceivable that jousting tournaments and other spectacles of the age would have taken place there, as a convenient tract of land on which to hold them.

As has been said, when the Bubonic Plague, the Black Death, raced through England in the 14th century, the Common filled a macabre "social" need — the bodies of those Bungayans who died from the epidemic were buried in a huge pit there. Another "social amenity" was the 18th century pest house.

But a much more cheerful amenity was also available via the Common, if not actually on it, at about the same time.

It was the facility for hot and cold baths, provided from a natural spring by the enterprising Mr John King. He found the source in what were then called the Vineyard Hills, now known as Bath Hills, just on the Norfolk side of the Common, but very much part of the Common landscape. Indeed the beauty of the Common would be the poorer without that beautiful backdrop.

An apothecary by profession, Mr King had searched for some time for a site to set up his cold bathing business, and he wrote later that he found it "in my own land, at the foot of a large and deep hill whose oblique height is not common; it's most curiously adorned with many sorts of trees standing in so handsome a manner as form of themselves a beautiful landscape; the opposite side is a fine, delightful stream (the Waveney), encompassing a large, spacious common whose prospect is little inferior to any."

Having established the facility, he had a footbridge erected over the river from the Common so that people could gain access from that direction. The bridge was "wide enough for a sedan chair to pass over," and for many years it was a fashionable resort for Suffolk gentry. Several marvellous cures were claimed of the cold bath, which measured 16ft by 10ft, and was built in 1728.

The advertising material for the therapeutic bath was fulsome — today we would probably say it was "over the top." This is a short extract:

...those lovely hills which encircle the flowery plain, variegated with all that can ravage the eye's astonishing sight, rise from the winding mazes of the River Waveney, encircled with the utmost the watery element is capable of producing. The steep and fertile vineyards, richly stored with the choicest plants from Burgundy, Champagne, Provence and whatever the East can furnish. Near the bottom of this is placed the grotto, or bath, beautifully decorated; on one side gardens, fruits, shady walks, and all the decorations of rural innocence.

As to the bathing there, 'tis a mixture of all that England, Paris or Rome could boast of, no one's refused a kind reception, honour and generosity reign throughout...

A Common Privilege

This is taken from Mr King's own *Essay on Hot and Cold Bathing*, published in 1737. The frontispiece, drawn by Thomas Bardwell, shows what appears to be a double gallows in the foreground of a panoramic view of Common with the Bath Hills beyond. Capital punishment was a sentence for a wide range of crimes in those days but there are no record of public executions having taken place on the Common and the structure may have been used for quite a different purpose. In fact, at this time, capital offences were usually heard at the Assizes; locally at Norwich and Bury St Edmunds, with the guilty being executed there in what were popular public spectacles.

Ethel Mann's book, *Old Bungay*, goes into more detail about Mr King's exploits, and Bungay as a spa.

The first recorded regular sporting event on the Common was horse racing, which probably began as early as 1700. There is evidence in newspaper advertisements that two-day meetings were held, with one taking place in April, 1718. Individual racing challenges, for bets, took place at other times.

It is likely that the smallpox outbreak put paid to some meetings in the middle of the 18th century. And there is evidence that at least as far as the individual challenges were concerned, they did not always take place with the permission of the Common Owners. When a race between two "capital horses" was advertised for May 1st, 1775, the Owners put the following letter in the papers:

We whose names are hereunto inscribed, being the proprietors of the Common in Bungay, and principal inhabitants of the town, do hereby give notice that we are determined, as far as in us lies, to prevent the horse race advertised, for the first day of May next, and to prosecute any persons that shall attempt having a race there at that or any future time.

It was signed by 14 owners, all prominent people: Thomas Manning, John van Kamp, Hen. Negus jun., W. Lewis, J. Reeve, John Cooper, Thomas Miller, Thomas Prentice, William Oldham, Edmund Jenney, Thomas Cotton jun., Chas. Cocking, Richard Harvey and Daniel Bonhote. The reason for the opposition is not clear, but the late E. A. Goodwyn, in his book on Bungay in the 18th century, *Elegance and Poverty*, writes:

Had some unauthorised outsider dared attempt to organise a race, or was there, as seems more likely, strong opposition to the use of the Common for this purpose? Race meetings brought trade to the town, and especially to the publicans. Local gentry generally supported them.

But they were by no means an unmixed blessing. Sharpers and pickpockets would infest the town, and probably prostitutes, too. They encouraged drunkenness. And what effect did they have on all the animals grazing on the Common — and on the grass then in spring growth? All the signatories had animals, probably horses, on the Common.

It is a good insight into the importance of the Common to the town, and to the Owners, at that time — protection of its primary use had to be given top priority.

So racing on the Common ceased for a while. Camping may have continued. This resembled a rough type of football, teams were usually, but by no means always, 12-a-side, and was governed only by the most basic of rules. Its origins were said to be ancient and peculiar to East Anglia, with the ball used varying in size from that of a cricket ball to something larger than a modern football. Camping matches were certainly held on the Common during the 18th and early 19th centuries, and one was advertised at The Bath House for ten-a-side on October 10th, 1741. But as these matches often covered a wide area, with pitches having only vague boundaries, one wonders if this, too, actually took place on the Common.

The matches were probably not welcomed by those running the Common, nor did they welcome prize-fights there. One contest, between the celebrated Ned Painter and Harry Sutton, on August 7th, 1818, attracted 15,000 people, despite rain, with spectators at the back perched on three circles of wagons in order to get a look. After a fight lasting one hour 40 minutes, and 15 rounds, Painter was the winner.

But when an attempt was made to arrange a contest on Outney Common on April 1st the following year, the Owners took steps to stop it. This time the spectators had already begun to assemble when a message came from the magistrates, sitting in the town that day, saying they would not permit the fight to take place there. It is likely that the action was at the request of the Common Owners, and almost certainly there were Owners among those on the Bench that day.

Meanwhile, racing eventually resumed on the Common, and was as popular as ever. There is a record of a meeting on September 17th, 1793, and on September 17th, 1827, a diary notes: "Bungay races resumed after many years, four thousand persons present."

At the meeting the following year there were nearly 10,000 on the Common to see the racing, and despite the limited transport of the times, they must have come from a very wide area. What is not clear is whether these meetings were flat races or over jumps, but they were undoubtedly a social as well as a sporting success. The *Norfolk Chronicle* records of that particular meeting:

It was very full and fashionably attended by not less than 10,000 people on the course which, from the extensiveness and undulating surface of Bungay Common, with surrounding picturesque scenery is, with the exception of Doncaster, considered the best in England.

This in itself suggests that Bungay races were attended by people from all over the country, including experts among the racing fraternity. It was praise indeed. And while it was "the sport of kings," or at the very least the landed gentry — the Earl of Stradbroke and Sir Edward Kerrison, MP, were stewards for the meeting on July, 1829 — ordinary people made up the bulk of the attendance.

Races at the time included the Town Plate, with £50 to the winner. In 1829 it was won by Mr Edwards' grey horse, Glory.

Surviving records of racing on the Common — it always took place on the Hards — are sketchy, and it may have lapsed again towards the middle of the century. But it was in the second half of the 19th century that sport really boomed on the Common, with golf, cricket, hockey, football and athletics all taking place there.

Racing was certainly part of that boom. There was a Bank Holiday meeting on August 6th, 1883, with a card of six races, and the organising committee comprised J. L. Gordon, Col. P. Bagot, Capt. F. Smith, R. Mann, W. Mann, George Durrant, J. Coker, Thomas Clarke, Charles Minns (also secretary and treasurer), Edgar Candler, B. Seaman and Thomas Smith.

Racing at this, and all previous meetings, was either over the flat or hurdles. Steeplechasing came to the Common just a few years later however, as an application to the Common Owners, considered on December 30th, 1887, shows. The minute book records:

On application of Charles C. Boycott of Flixton on behalf of the Bungay Racing Committee, it was agreed to allow them to make a steeplechase course, including water jumps. Boycott agreed to do nothing that was detrimental to the present race course (the existing flat race course). Fee of £5 a year agreed, excluding an erection of a stand for the races.

So steeple-chasing came to Bungay Common at a time when it was becoming well used for a variety of sporting activities, and another significant application came before the Owners almost exactly a year later, on December 31st, 1888. They accepted the request from Mr. R. C. Mann to set up golf links on the Common, at a rent of £2 2s a year — and Bungay Golf Club, later to become the Bungay and Waveney Valley Golf Club, was born. At that same meeting the Owners approved an application by Mr Charles Garneys to lay a cricket ground, at 5s a year rent.

Cricket had been played on the Common for years with some regularity, with an organised club in existence, but it did not stop at cricket. *The Norwich Mercury* of September 16th, 1865, records:

The committee of the cricket club have arranged a series of athletics sports to take place upon the Common, on the afternoon of the 20th, when prizes to the amount of £10 will be given to the successful competitors in swimming, jumping, throwing and other matches. The band of the 4th Suffolk Rifles will be in attendance,

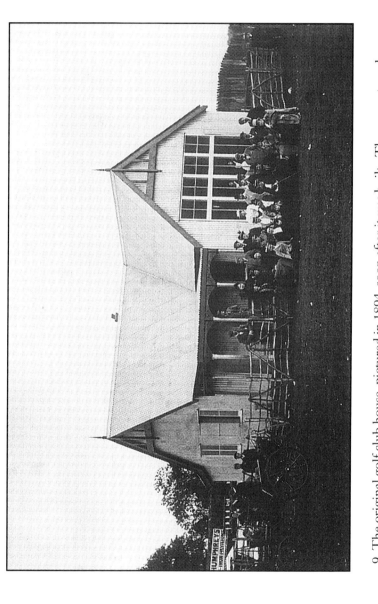

9. The original golf club house, pictured in 1894, soon after it was built. The present modern clubhouse is on the same site.

10. Presentations at the golf club house on the Common around the turn of the century.

11. A view over the Common, taken in the early part of this century from Bath Hills.

GOLF ON BUNGAY COMMON.

H.S. Smith, Photo.

12. Golf on the Common in the 1920s. Note the sparse vegetation compared to today.

and we learn that the principal shop keepers and others have agreed to close their places of business for half a day.

So the townspeople and others from a wide area flocked to the Common to enjoy a half-day off, and the sports. The event attracted several thousand spectators, and the Rev. J. J. Owen, a master at the grammar school, was judge. Herbert Hartcup, later to become Town Reeve, won the mile event. The swimming, of course, took place in the River Waveney.

The sports became an annual event, and the third annual athletics sports were on September 8th, 1867. This time 3000 people attended, and enjoyed 16 events, including the pole vault, in which the winner, a Mr. Howard, cleared 9ft.

By this time football had evolved from the camp ball activities, and the Common was a regular venue for that too, with the pitch usually sited in front of where the golf clubhouse now is, although its location did vary.

One of the earliest organised teams to play there was the Chaucer Press team, from the printing works which is now Clays Ltd. It formed a team in 1885, and played regularly on the Common. In 1892 it was good enough to win the Suffolk Junior Cup, beating Brantham Athletic 4-1 in the final at Portman Road, Ipswich.

So impressed were Ipswich Town, who played (and still do) at Portman Road, with the Bungay team that they arranged a match with them — on Bungay Common, on April 16th, 1892. A notable side indeed to play at Bungay, though of course not a Premier League side in those days.

What would sport in Bungay have done without the Common in that period of the late 19th century when sport was emerging as such a leading leisure pursuit in Victorian England? There were other areas in the town to play, but it was Outney Common to which people turned first when wanting wide green spaces, and of course it was the only practical place for golf and racing.

The Common Owners accepted this use readily at that stage, and in 1891 agreed to put iron seats there for the use of the public. The fashion of going for walks, or constitutionals, was highly popular with the Victorians, and the less energetic of them would have found the seats a great boon when stopping for a rest.

Both golf and steeplechase racing became quickly established, with jumps being erected and greens laid. Two race meetings a year were held, usually in the spring and autumn, always attracting several thousand people, and horses and riders from all over the country. Pony and galloway races were also organised there.

It was not too long before the race committee erected a grandstand on the Common for the convenience of the more affluent spectators — the working class people made do with farm carts to get a good view of the action. The grandstand was put up in 1895, and greatly added to the atmosphere and bustle of the occasion, which was good for the town. The pounding of hooves around the course (which was circular and went right down to the bottom of The Hards), the cheering of the crowds, the activities of the bookies, and the excitement of the children made race days much looked forward to, a highlight of Bungay's year.

The finish was in front of the grandstand, which stood with its back close to the " cliff" which now leads down to the lake. Later a second grandstand was built alongside it, both fixed buildings which were in addition to temporary seating and enclosures put up for each meeting.

Around the turn of the century, hockey was yet another sport played on the Common, with a tent erected for changing accommodation. St Mary's School, situated in Earsham Street, used it as a playing field later on, with the hockey pitch marked out in front of the golf clubhouse. It was used until the school closed in 1966. Bungay Grammar School also used it when the school was situated in Earsham Street, where the Post Office now is.

Many people have swum or paddled in the river on the Common over the centuries. The Waveney was the only place to swim locally, and on hot days it no doubt got quite crowded, particularly in the area where the children's playground now is, near the bypass bridge. When the railway was built the line ran over a bridge at the

BUNGAY
STEEPLECHASES
AND
HURDLE RACES
(UNDER NATIONAL HUNT RULES)

THURSDAY & FRIDAY
APRIL 22 & 23, 1920

Prices of Admission on Days of Races:

Stand and Paddock, 20/- per Day; 35/- Two Days
(including Tax).
Second Ring, 6/- (including Tax).
Carriages or Motors, to Course 25/-
To Enclosure (extra), 15/-

Clerk of the Course: Mr. A. S. MANNING, Newmarket,
Secretary: Mr. GORDON BARRATT, Bungay.

13. Poster advertising the two-day Bungay Races event on Outney
Common in April, 1920.

14. Bungay boys watching the races on Outney Common in the 1920s from Mr Gordon Barrett's lorry.

15. A panoramic view of the crowds at Bungay Races in 1909 as they wait for the next race. The two grandstands are clearly visible.

PUBLISHED BY AUTHORITY.

BUNGAY RACES

TUESDAY JULY THE 7TH, 1885.

COMMITTEE:—

W. Hartcup, Esq.   Col. P. Bagot,   Captn. H. J. Hartcup.   Captn. F. Smith.
R. Mann, Esq.   Mr. J. P. Coker,   Mr. G. Durrant.   Mr. T. Clarke.
Mr. Chas. Draper.   Mr. Chas. Minns.

Judge :—Mr. G. Durrant.   Starter:—J. Wittrick.   Clerks of the Course :—Police.
Clerk of the Scales :—Mr. J. Norman.   Hon. Sec. and Treas. :—Mr. C. Minns, Bungay.

1.30.—THE TRADESMENS' PLATE,

An open Race, for Horses to carry 11 stone.   About 2 Miles over 5 Flights of Hurdles.
Winner £10.   Second £1.   Entrance Fee 10s. 6d.

1. Mr. C. R. Packer's ch.h. "Irishman," light blue and yellow.
2. Mr. W. Foulger's "Little Tim," black body and cap.
3. Mr. Hy. Blyth's b.m. "Mariza," chocolate and pink.

2.0.—THE WAVENEY STAKES,

An open Race for Galloways, not exceeding 14hds. 2in., to carry 10st.
(7lbs. allowed for every inch).   About 1½ Mile on the Flat.
Winner £8.   Second £1.   Entrance Fee 10s. 6d.

1. Mr. E. S. Taylor's b.h. "Bittern," blue and yellow hoops, white cap and red spots.
2. Mr. E. Slater's "Musical Joe," black and red.
3. Mr. Brown's b.m. "Disturbance," mauve body and amber sleeves.
4. Mr. Jas. Cleveland's b.h. "Idle Boy," crimson body, blue cap and sleeves.
5. Mr. Geo. Archer's gr.m. "Snowflight," black body, white sleeves, and red cap.
6. Mr. Dobson's r.m. "Florence," magpie.

2.45.—THE UPLAND STAKES,

An open Race for Horses to carry 11st.   Winner once at this Meeting 14lbs. extra.
About 2 Miles on the flat.   Winner £10.   Second £1.   Entrance Fee 10s. 6d.

1. Mr. F. G. Playford's ch.g. "Forecast," scarlet, white sleeves, black cap.
2. Mr. E. Slater's "Musical Joe," black and red.
3. Mr. W. Foulger's "Little Tim," black body and cap.
4. Mr. Brown's "Disturbance," mauve body and amber sleeves.

3.30.—THE NORFOLK AND SUFFOLK HUNT CUP,

Value £35.   For Horses that have regularly hunted with some established Pack of Hounds in Norfolk or Suffolk.   4 yr. old 10st. 7lbs.   5 yr. old 11st. 8lbs.   6 yr. old and aged 12st. 3lbs.
About 2½ Miles over 5 Flights of Hurdles.   Winner £30.   Second £5.
Entrance Fee £2 2s., which must be accompanied by a Certificate from a Master of Hounds.

1. Mr. Hy. Blyth's b.m. "Mariza," chocolate and pink.
2. Mr. F. G. Playford's ch g. "Forecast," scarlet, white sleeves, and black cap.
3. Mr. Jno. Printer's blk m. "Bridget," blue and white.
4. Mr. C. R. Packer's ch.h. "Irishman," light blue and yellow.
5. Mr. Cross's b.g. "Brompton," black and cherry sleeves and cap.
6. Mr. Tunaley's b.m. "Sweet Rose" yellow body, black sleeves, and maroon cap.

16. The race card for one of the early Bungay race meetings, in 1885.

17. The scene at Bungay Races in about 1909.

18. Busy scene at the races on Outney Common in 1906, clearly showing the fashions of the time, and the vantage points used to view the steeplechase and hurdle races.

19. Taking the waterjump at Bungay Races in 1904, in front of the huge crowds gathered on the slopes. The site is where the golf club practice range now is, on the west side of the Common.

20. Coming home to win in front of the packed grandstands, once a familiar site on Outney Common. This one was the Whitsun meeting of 1909.

same spot, and the location became known to Bungay families simply as The Train Bridge.

After the formation of the Bungay Urban District Council in 1910, one of the early moves towards leisure facilities was the provision of a bathing hut for the public. The UDC rented a site at Toby's Hole, a few hundred yards down river from the Train Bridge. The erection of the hut was organised by a sub-committee of the Bungay General Committee of the Coronation (of George V) in 1912. The committee seems to have become the bathing hut committee, elected by the UDC, and there was a shelter as well as a hut.

In 1913 Henry Rushmer, Clerk to the Common Owners, had to write to the UDC reminding it that two years rent for the site was outstanding, though it appears the UDC paid promptly after receiving the letter! The facilities remained there for many years and many Bungay people remember using them.

Chapter 8
Sir Alfred Munnings

This was a plunge into the most vividly coloured phase of life I had so far seen. I had known horse sales in Norwich, local races and regattas; but what were they compared to this vast fair and meeting combined on Bungay Common?

So wrote Sir Alfred Munnings, the Suffolk artist described as the greatest horse painter since George Stubbs, on his first visit to Bungay Common, and the race meeting there, at the turn of the century. It was that visit, says the foreword on the dust jacket on the first part of his autobiography, that first aroused his interest in race horses, jockeys in silks, gypsy caravans and all the motley excitement of the race course that were typical of the Bungay meetings.

In that book, *An Artist's Life*, Munnings waxed lyrical about that day his friend took him, by train along the Waveney Valley line, to the first race meeting he had attended — the very day on which he heard he had had his first work (two oil paintings) accepted by the Royal Academy:

There were roundabouts, shooting galleries, swing-boats and coconut shies; large eating- and drinking-tents, flags flying and thousands of oranges blazing on stalls in the sun. I had never seen such droves of ponies and gypsy lads.

But all this, with music and noise, died away and dwindled to nothing when I saw the thoroughbred horses and jockeys — professional gentlemen and riders...in bright silk colours, going off down the course.

So imagine me, gaping at the scene now thrown at me all at once. The peaceful School of Art, the smelly artists' room, faded away, and I began to live! I had never imagined such a sight, although my imagination went as far as prairie fires.

And so race followed race, steeple-chase or hurdle, while I stood either at the open ditch or water-jump seeing such colour and action as I had never dreamed of.

Munnings took little persuading to return for a second day of the race meeting the following day. Of that he wrote, in more phrases as colourful as his art:

The noise of the fair was as great and the sun on the striped awnings and oranges as flaming and brilliant as before, the turf on the Common springy and full of scents, with skylarks above.

Thus ended two great days in my life, and soon after I did a set of four pastels — the jumps, the finish and all the rest — and sold them for what I thought was a lot of money.

Some time later the same friend took Munnings to a race meeting at Epsom, where he watched his first Derby race from the stands. Though he enjoyed the experience, he observed in his autobiography: " That crowded, gigantic occasion at Epsom had not the colour of Bungay..."

Much later Norfolk author Jean Goodman, in her book on the life of Munnings, wrote of that visit to Bungay Common which made such an impression on the then young artist: " It was a heady experience; a plunge into the most colourful phase of life at the very moment he was dazed with the joy of knowing that, at last, he could truly describe himself as a painter."

As to those four pastels he did of Bungay Races, they are now valuable works. But he did others as well, and it is certain he returned to Bungay Common, and the races, in ensuing years.

One of his works, in oils and called Bungay Races, measures 13.5 inches by 17.5 inches, is dated 1901 and is currently at the Hunterian Art Gallery at the University of Glasgow. It was bought by Dr Charles Hepburn in 1964 and was bequeathed to the gallery in 1971. In 1928 it had formed part of a Munnings exhibition at Norwich Castle Museum, when it was loaned by Mr Arthur Gibbs.

Another oil, also called Bungay Races and measuring 12 inches by 16 inches, dated 1902 and inscribed on the reverse, was sold by Sotheby's in a New York sale on October 28th, 1982, for 40,000 dollars. A drawing, called Band of 7th Hussars, Bungay Races, and dated 1900, was among those on show at the Norwich exhibition.

Munnings also did paintings at Bungay Horse Fair, but that was not normally held on the Common — it was at Skinner's Meadow, or Fairstead Meadow, at St John's Road.

Chapter 9
The Dr Beard Case & the Problems of the First World War

There's osier beds and willowherb and sand;
Bright buttercups and daisies all abound.
There's gentle slopes, and hollows, narrow paths;
Contented people out for Sunday walks.

And yes, the Waveney, that gentle stream,
A loving ribbon of eternity,
That cradles Bungay Common to its breast
In slow, relaxing ripples of repose.

The 19th century ended with more controversy as the Common Owners finally lost their patience with those who continued to take liberties and abuse the Common facilities. They took someone to court — but it did not turn out as they had hoped.

The gates to the Common were always locked punctually at 8pm, but many people in the town were not happy with the arrangement. And the Owners were not happy about horses being ridden on the Common for leisure, as opposed to organised race meetings.

Dr Thomas Beard, who lived close to the Common at Waveney Terrace, in Outney Road, was not happy with either arrangement, and from time to time took his horse on the Common for exercise. He had caused damage to the gates at the Outney Road entrance on one occasion, and when he repeated the damage a second time in December, 1896, the Owners decided to act.

Their minute book of December 8th of that year records that at a special meeting called to discuss the matter, it was decided " to take out a summons against Thomas Beard of Waveney Terrace, for wilful damage to the gates at the Outney Road entrance to the Common on two occasions."

Cases got to court much quicker in those days, and the *Eastern Daily Press* of January 1st, 1897, and the *East Suffolk Gazette* on January 5th contained reports of the hearing. Henry Rider Haggard (author of King Solomon's Mines and other classics) was the presiding magistrate at Bungay Court, and he and his colleagues heard Dr. Beard, through his solicitor, Mr. J. C. Chittock, plead not guilty to the charge of wilfully damaging the gate to the Common by sawing it through to let his horse off the Common on December 5th, 1896.

Henry Rushmer, Clerk to the Common Owners, told the court that on November 18th he saw Dr. Beard's servant with a horse on the Common, and told him the Owners objected to the Common being ridden on. The man returned home.

Mr Rushmer wrote to Dr. Beard on December 1st explaining that eight or nine years previously people did have the right to ride on the Common by paying a fee of £5 a year, but because of the number of applications that came in, a special meeting of the Common Reeves decided that permission should no longer be given.

Dr. Beard wrote back saying he thought the action of the Owners was illegal.

Mr Rushmer continued that on December 3rd he saw the horse on the Common again, and afterwards saw the gate with the head cut through. On the Monday another part of the gate was cut. The cost of repair was 7s. He told the court the Common gates were locked at night to prevent trespassers, or cattle straying.

After contacting Dr Beard again, he received another letter from him which said: " In consequence of your illegal orders to shut my horse on the Common, I found it necessary to saw one bar of the chained gate in order to get my horse through. I was careful to avoid unnecessary damage. I beg to say that I shall continue to ride on horseback on Bungay Common, taking such measures to take my horse off as the circumstances of the case may warrant."

George Everett, known as "Friday," employed by the Owners, told the court he saw Dr. Beard cut the gate on the 5th but not on the 3rd. He had seen several people riding on the Common, and when he spoke to them they took it "very unkindly."

Mr. Chittock argued that if this was a civil case there could be many witnesses to call on the question of right. He based his claim on public foot and horse way, inhabitants, owners, occupiers and a right to free and lawful use of the Common for all sport, including horse exercise, and various games.

A number of people gave evidence of riding on the Common — one, Thomas Parrington, aged 88, of Earsham, saying he rode there as far back as 1824, and his right was never challenged. Mr. Henry Wightman, by that time three times Town Reeve of Bungay, a draper in the town and a Suffolk County Councillor, said he had used the Common for riding, walking and perambulators. He had had no permission, objection, or charge of obstruction. He had seen other people repeatedly riding there.

Leather cutter Samuel Nursey and corn merchant William Walker (also a former and future Town Reeve at the time) gave similar evidence.

Some of the evidence at the hearing related to the deeds to the Common, which Mr Rushmer was unable to produce. And he admitted, when pressed by Mr Rider Haggard, that the Owners did not dispute the right of people to walk on the Common.

At the end, Mr Rider Haggard summed up the case in this way:

The bench has heard the evidence that has been put before them, and considered it carefully. In the opinion of the bench, sufficient evidence of the claim of right has been produced to oust the jurisdiction of this court. The case therefore, if it proceeds, must be decided elsewhere. So far as this court is concerned, it stands dismissed.

The *Eastern Daily Press* reported that "a large amount of interest was manifested in the case throughout the town and neighbourhood, resulting in a large attendance at court." And when the decision was announced it was greeted with loud applause from the large gathering, who certainly saw it as something of a victory for the local belief that Bungay residents did have a right to use the Common — a right which they felt was suggested by its very name.

The case was not taken to a civil court by the Owners, but it did lead them to have another careful look at how the Common was run. Not for the first time they decided, as recorded in the minutes of their meeting of January 15th, 1897:

In view of the decision by magistrates in Dr Beard's case, it was agreed to obtain a provisional order for the future control and management of the Common.

They obviously had second thoughts, however, because seven weeks later they simply agreed to appoint seven reeves " to undertake the management as heretofore." One new appointment, on March 11th, 1897, was George Everett as a stock bailiff.

The outbreak of the First World War in 1914 brought yet another use for the Common — and yet more problems for everyone, including the Bungay school in Wingfield Street.

Large areas of the Common nearest the town were quickly transformed into military camps as the Army commandeered it, and thousands of soldiers were billeted there. As early as December, 1914, the golf club was complaining that the troops, with their horses, were doing unnecessary racing and riding, causing a lot of damage to the course and the fairways. A letter went from the Common Owners to the commanding officer telling him of the complaint, and saying they felt the riding was over and above normal drill.

The club tried to carry on under the new handicap, but its activities were inevitably curtailed. The final blow came in May, 1916, when the 62nd West Riding division of the Royal Engineers moved in to set up seven camps of 1700 horses and 1800 men. The golf clubhouse was taken over for the officers' mess, and that was that — the club was discontinued.

With other troops already there the Common was home for thousands of men, horses and their accompanying paraphernalia, bringing a nightmare for the Owners. Mr Rushmer resigned as Clerk on January 13th, 1915, through ill health after 32 years' service, and perhaps the presence of the troops had something to do with this. Mr. Alfred Cocks took his place.

Trying to run a working Common from which people got a livelihood while it was occupied by the military must have been an almost impossible task, and the Owners tried to make a stand. Their chairman, Mr. A. C. Smith, told Lieutenant A. E. Gerald Collins that the Common was "owned by private persons and the public only had a right to walk on it."

But Owners and public alike could do little, as manœuvres there included digging trenches for bomb-throwing practise.

While many people simply accepted the presence of the troops as a necessary part of the war effort and put up with it, the activities were a huge attraction and excitement to one section of the community — children. Many would go there at every opportunity to watch them, talk to the men, and maybe get the odd souvenir to cherish.

Evidence of this attraction is in the Bungay Board School log book. Records of truancy increased during the war, and a typical entry was:

23/10/16 — Arthur Ford: offence — taking little brother on the Common all Monday, and telling lies. Punishment — one (stroke of the cane) on each hand, four on trousers.

A severe punishment, one would think, but it did not deter the same boy skipping school a week later to go on the Common. On that occasion the teacher went to fetch him at 12.15pm, and administered two strokes of the cane on each hand and several on the seat.

The most enlightening entry in the book by headmaster C. Barnes was on August 7th, 1916, against the name of Frank Money: *This boy has twice truanted, spending one whole day on the Common, and ever since the soldiers have been here has been rude, disobedient and troublesome. I have promised him a caning every time he causes an upset in his class, which is very often.*

The Dr. Beard Case

Truancy continued, however — the temptation for young boys to watch the troops training must have been overpowering, and there must have been an element of education in it.

The Common Owners gave little thought to that. They had to see the soldiers did not abuse their welcome, but there were advantages, particularly as the war drew to a close. Not only did they get an additional £5 annual rent for the compound built to contain German prisoners-of-war, the prisoners were also put to work on such tasks as clearing reeds from the river.

Damage to the Common was inevitable, and the Owners put in a claim to the War Office for £324 19s 3d as compensation for damage in 1916, once peace was declared. The War Office offered what seemed a paltry £49 7s 6d, though accepted a claim of £98 7s 6d for damage in 1917.

Mr. Cocks was instructed to tell the War Office of the Owners' dissatisfaction at the offer, but to accept £49 19s 3d if no better offer was made, though it appears little headway was made on this. The golf club and the race committee put in separate hefty claims, again disputed by the War Office. The golf club got £50 for damage to the course, but when the Army finally vacated the clubhouse on April 7th, 1919, claims were put in for "dilapidations," and missing crockery and glass. There is no record that this claim was met.

Much damage was caused to the Common during the war by bomb damage in a Zeppelin raid, according to Charles Hancy, who sadly died in 1993. Many cattle were also killed when, it seems, the bombs meant for the military encampment fell on grazing animals instead. Mr Hancy recalls helping the horse slaughterer, Jack Wards, to clear the dead animals, and kill those which were wounded.

Seven bombs were dropped in all, Mr. Hancy remembered, and left holes so big "you could put a horse in." He helped Mr. Wards at his work all one Sunday, and got £1 for his efforts.

Mr. Hancy, who was 93, had clear memories of how the Common and the goings system operated in the early days of the century, and they are worth recording here. He remembers, for instance, that one commonage represented two head of cattle, or two goings, and that at that time some were still attached to properties — two cottages on the Drift at Outney Road had papers confirming that. Others, he said, had been attached to other houses and cottages, but people parted with them to pay off their debts. He recalled that one grocer took several in settlement of grocery bills.

After the spring growth, cattle were allowed onto the Lows and the Haycroft, the pasture on the west side of the Hards, on the Thursday before May 12th. Goings would have been booked the previous October, at 4s each, which enabled cattle to be grazed on the Hards throughout the winter, mainly for exercise and water.

Mr. Hancy's recollection was that those who owned the commonages did not have to pay to graze their cattle on the Common in the summer. Those who owned them but did not want to use them for their own cattle would let them — a job put in the hands of an auctioneer who would let them all on one day for the season.

The hiring would be for an average rent — "on the average" was Mr. Hancy's phrase for it — for Bungay people. If some commonages let for £4, and others for £3, Bungay people would get theirs for £3. His father hired several each year.

Another interesting piece of information Mr. Hancy came up with was that profits from the running of the Common, after all expenses were paid, were used to provide coal for the poor people of Bungay at Christmas, and late autumn. He recalls helping bag it up at the coalyard at Bungay station, and helping to deliver it round the town on a wagon.

It was tales such as that which led Mr. Hancy to tell George Ewart Evans, as recorded in his book *The Days That We Have Seen,* that "there isn't such a thing as a Common Owner. All they own is a piece of paper just entitling them to feed."

The war finally over, life on Outney Common gradually returned to normal. Golf resumed, local teams used the football pitch again, racing got under way, and with the Army gone, people enjoyed the area for recreation in general once more. Some people can even remember open air services being held on the Common towards the end of the war, and after it was over.

Two familiar Common landmarks were put in place in the following few years. One, in 1922, was a unispan bridge over the river by the old, now demolished, Mill House, linking the Common with Ditchingham. It was erected by the Town Reeve of the day, H. N. Rumsby, who ran an ironworks in the town, and replaced the old wooden bridge which had been there for at least 100 years, and which was in a bad state of repair. A plaque set into the bridge's footway denotes Mr. Rumsby's gift.

And in 1926 the Common Owners agreed to spend up to £35 on new entrance gates at the Outney Road approach. The wrought iron gates can still be seen there today at what is now the entrance to Clay's lorry park.

Air displays and flights were another recreational attraction for which the Common was an ideal site. The Owners allowed the Haycroft to be used by the British Hospital's Air Pageants Ltd "for aviation demonstrations and passenger flights" in 1933. And in 1936 British Empire Air Displays mounted an air display on the Common. Large crowds were attracted to both events.

21. George Baldry, who lived at the Mill House, on the Ditchingham side of the River Waveney at Outney Common, pictured with his wife in 1947. The Mill House is in the picture on the right.

22. The picturesque Bath House, viewed from the Common in the early 1900s.

On The Waveney, Bungay.

23. Boating on the Waveney around the Common was always a popular recreation. These two ladies had just hired their boat from George Baldry at the Mill House, which can be seen in the background.

24. The Mill House, with the bridge built by George Baldry,
linking it to the "island' on the east side of the Common.

Chapter 10
The 1920s
Pumped Water & the Suffolk Show

Then you lift your wide, wide wings -
Oh, it is wonderful to see
The majesty of that slow, slow flight.
Yes, you are the lord of the marsh for me.

From *The Heron*, by Dorothy Stevens

With the First World War over, Bungay Urban District Council set about improving the town's amenities, and turned its thoughts to a piped water supply for as many residents as possible. In seeking a site for a waterworks, the obvious place was Outney Common, where boreholes had been sunk during the war to serve the troops encamped there.

An area of just under 17 acres in the centre of The Hards was identified as the best location, and test bores were sunk in September, 1922. Six weeks later the Common Reeves considered a formal application by the town's water supply committee to buy the land, which would be enclosed by a " substantial fence," with gates in it to allow golfers and the public access, and to prevent cattle getting in.

The Urban District Council was also in correspondence with the Ministry of Agriculture and the Ministry of Health on the matter of compulsory purchase of the land. In one letter to the Ministry of Agriculture the Town Clerk, Mr Percy Sprake, wrote:

The public have rights of walking on the whole Common, but the rights of depasturing stock belong to about 60 persons, who also claim to be the Owners of the soil of the Common.

The question of compensating the Common Owners has been discussed with the district council but no agreement as to the amount to be paid can be arrived at, owing mainly to the fact that the Common Owners claim to be entitled to the soil, whereas the council considers that they are entitled to the rights of depasturing stock only.

But in another letter to the Ministry, two weeks later, on January 29th, Mr Sprake wrote:

I am of the opinion that my council can acquire the soil voluntarily under the Public Health Acts, and subsequently extinguish the common rights under the Land Clauses Consolidation Act, 1845, as I think there is no doubt whatever the soil of the Common is vested in the Common Owners. Some members of the council dispute the common ownership of the soil because the soil was not vested in them originally. Formerly the only rights conveyed to the Common Owners were the rights of depasturing stock, but in many recent cases the documents of transfer have conveyed undivided interests in the soil of the Common.

Mr Sprake quoted the instance of the sale of the land by the Common Owners to the Great Eastern Railway in 1864, with the company paying the whole of the purchase money to the Owners. He also pointed out that in 1879 the Queen's Bench division of the High Court decided that Outney Common was rateable to the Poor Rate, and thus considered that the soil was vested in the Common Owners, as a right of common itself was not rateable. His letter also said:

No doubt the ownership of the soil was vested originally in the Lord of the Manor, the Duke of Norfolk, but all rights which he may have had have been lost many years since.

These were details and views that were to have significant effect nearly 60 years later, and demonstrate again that at that time many people in Bungay felt strongly that the Owners should not claim ownership of the Common, despite the views of the Town Clerk.

With the Ministry telling the council it had no jurisdiction to determine the ownership of the Common, except through a provisional order under the Commons Act of 1876, the council decided to acquire two goings, so that it was in the same position as other Common Owners. They were bought from Mr. Harry Rumsby for £70, and in buying them the council implicitly accepted that the Common was owned by a group of individuals, of which Mr Rumsby was one.

Legal obstacles having been cleared, the sale of the land by the Owners to the Urban District Council went through, and the Bungay waterworks was built, and enclosed with a fence of iron railings. It remains the only permanent building, apart from the old clubhouse, on the whole of Outney Common.

There was a debate on the cost of the land sold, with the Owners originally asking £50 an acre. But they eventually settled for £504 11s 3d, as recorded in their minutes of August 4th, 1925.

The waterworks went into commission in 1924. The provision of a piped domestic water supply was a huge step forward for Bungay and its people, and the programme of connecting homes to it progressed quickly. It took some time to reach all homes, however, and more remote places continued to rely on hand pumps for many years.

The 1920s also saw the Suffolk Show, the county's great farming and social occasion, finally come to Bungay. The town had lobbied for some time for it to be staged there, and when the Suffolk Agricultural Association finally agreed, Outney Common was the only site on which it could be held.

It took place on June 6th and 7th, 1929. It was the 51st Suffolk Show, and completely transformed the front part of the Common with sheds, marquees, stands, pens, rings and other buildings being erected over the three weeks leading up to the opening day. The town, led by the Town Reeve, Alfred Cocks, who was also Clerk to the Common Owners, was anxious that the event should be a success, and it was. Entries came from all over the country to the Common, and numbers compared well with previous shows — 245 horses, 248 cattle, 152 sheep, 112 swine, 2000 implements, and 20 entries in dairy competitions.

Unfortunately the sun did not shine on Bungay that June. The morning of the first day of the show was overcast, and it rained

25. Finches Well, a spot on the River Waveney on the Common, pictured in 1915. Note the bathing hut on the left, and the rowing boat on the river.

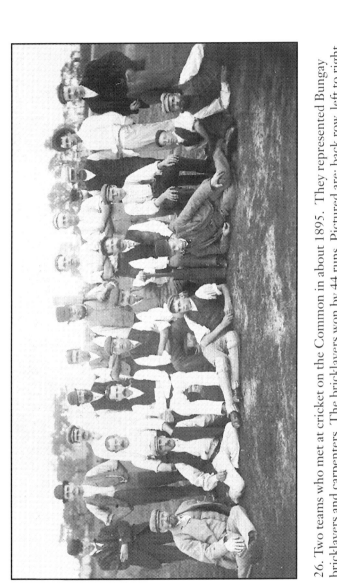

26. Two teams who met at cricket on the Common in about 1895. They represented Bungay bricklayers and carpenters. The bricklayers won by 44 runs. Pictured are: back row, left to right – unknown, Fred Brighton, Jeremiah Brighton, Chats Woodrow, James Brighton (capt.), H. Leech, Charles Brighton, Sam Codling, John Doe, Eli Honeywood. Middle – William Read, George Rowe, Lively Hood, Arthur Botwright (capt.), George Davis, James Davey. Front – Robert Biles, Charles Reynolds (Fox), J Phillips, Charles Denny Botwright, George Chandles, H Martin (Hixie).

27. The Bungay Carnival Band in action at a well supported event on the Common, circa 1925.

28. Work progressing on the building of the water pumping station on the Common. It was completed in 1924, and officially opened on December 12th that year.

incessantly throughout the afternoon, weather which undoubtedly affected the attendance — 1476 up to 2pm, and 2059 for the afternoon. Things improved for the second day, and by noon over 4000 people had flocked to the Common to enjoy the exhibitions and entertainment.

Generally the event reflected well on Bungay. The *East Anglian Daily Times* report commented:

This result is especially flattering to the town and district of Bungay, and particularly those who were responsible for the invitation of this year's visit of the association to this historic neighbourhood. It was the first occasion the Suffolk Agricultural Association has ventured to Bungay, and the fact that those responsible for the invitation had no misgivings is shown in the splendid entries...

What also stands to the credit of Bungay and the Waveney Valley is the fact that there was such enthusiasm for the coming of the great Suffolk Show into their neighbourhood, that they responded so heartily to the appeal for funds that a sum well in excess of £500 was subscribed. If, therefore, any town in the county deserved to have complete success associated with the annual event, then it was the town of Bungay.

Secretary Mr Will K. Bond overcame what seemed to be insurmountable difficulties in organisation, and the *East Anglian Daily Times* said "one of the most successful shows in Suffolk has been held on one of the smallest sites in recent years."

The hard-backed catalogue for the show covered 296 pages and cost 1s 6d.

Chapter 11
The 1930s — and more controversies

Mr George Baldry ran the boathouse in those days. We could hire a boat or a flat skip and row up and down the river. His wife made cakes and tea and sold sweets at the kitchen door...As kids in those days we spent all day on the Common in the holidays, with jam sandwiches and a bottle of lemonade.
Edie Rainger, daughter of Common Bailiff, Broomy Baldry.

S ince the establishment of regular steeplechase racing on the Common, the Bungay Steeplechase Committee had made no charge for admission to the meetings. The people of Bungay in any event had always closely protected what they felt was their right to free access there.

But with racing popular, and attracting thousands of people from a wide area, the committee wanted to maximise its income from the events, which cost a lot to stage, and in 1922, secretary Gordon Barratt wrote to the Common Owners asking for permission for gate money to be charged on race days.

Mindful of what local feeling might be, however, the letter, dated December 11th, suggested the gate money be shared equally between the committee, the Owners and the Urban District Council and added:

They (the committee) would also suggest, so as to overcome any hostile feelings from the inhabitants of Bungay, that the inhabitants should be admitted free, either at the same gate, or the Broad Street gate.

The Owners agreed to the idea, though it was limited to a period of not more than 12 days a year, and things seemed to go smoothly for some years — until 1933, when the race committee, which had run into financial difficulties, took steps to get Bungay people to pay too.

It outlined the reasons in a letter to the *Beccles and Bungay Journal,* published on November 19th, and signed by the chairman, Thomas Cook, and secretary Sidney Owles. They asked the people of Bungay to agree to be charged for admission to the races to help get the committee out of debt. Losses in eight years had amounted to £850, and they said unless support was received for the races the meetings would become a thing of the past.

"The committee feels sure that all sportsmen in Bungay would extremely regret the abandonment of this sporting fixture on the famous old Common, which has considerably added to the fame and prosperity of their town in the past..." it said.

The Common Owners duly sanctioned the change, but a challenge was no doubt expected and it came from Mr. Cecil Clay. He was affronted that Bungay people should be asked to pay to use what they felt was their Common, and referred the matter to the Commons and Open Spaces Preservation Society, whose secretary, Sir Lawrence Chubb, took a keen interest in the case. On October 31st, 1934, he came to Bungay for a meeting with the Common Reeves, the race committee and the Urban District Council.

He told them that until the Law of Property Act of 1925 was passed the public had no legal right at all to wander over the Common or stray from the public footpath over it.'But the Act gave them that right, providing no "limitations and conditions" of use of the Common had been sanctioned by Parliament. He advised the Owners that they could apply for a "limitations and conditions" scheme, or the Urban District Council could apply for a regulation scheme, which would give it control of the Common. It would have to maintain it, but would not receive any financial benefit from it.

Sir Lawrence recommended the "limitations and conditions" option, and the Owners and the Urban District Council went away to assess their positions.

It led to the Owners, now under the chairmanship of Mr. H. N. Rumsby, coming close to taking what would have been a momentous step in the history of Outney Common, and one which would have had far reaching effects on how it was run. They talked about selling the entire Common — all 300 goings — to the National Trust for a total of £12,750.

Initially, the idea must have had considerable appeal to the Owners from a financial point of view, and at a special meeting on March 14th, 1935, they asked their legal adviser, Mr. Geoffrey Sprake, to continue his negotiations with Sir Lawrence Chubb with a view to the National Trust buying the Common.

While these discussions continued, the Common Reeves agreed that the Little Common could be sold to Richard Clay Ltd. for £1500 if the sale of the main Common went ahead.

But things did not work out as the Owners had hoped. At a meeting at the Ministry of Agriculture with Sir Lawrence, Mr. Sprake learned that Outney Common was not a common within the meaning of the Law of Property Act, so no "limitations and conditions" scheme could be put forward. But it meant the Common could be enclosed on certain days and charges made for admission, even though it was a common as far as the Enclosure Act of 1899 and the Commons Act of 1876 were concerned.

When the maze of the different meanings of the different Acts was explained to the Owners, they decided to hold fire on any decision on selling the Common. They felt it would be premature to take any steps towards a scheme under the 1876 Commons Act which would mean their acting as conservators of the Common, retaining management of it, perhaps with the Urban District Council as joint conservators. They took the advice to wait for a Bill which would amend the Act — but it seems that such a Bill never went through Parliament, and the idea of a sale to the National Trust simply faded away.

The Steeplechase Committee was left free to charge entry to the races, though many Bungay people were far from happy with the situation, and it was something that was to be challenged again in later years. Meanwhile, negotiations began again for the sale of part of the Little Common to Clays.

Three years later an even more controversial proposal was put forward which threatened the very existence of Outney Common, and caused heated debate in homes, meetings and council chamber alike.

It is probably true to say that most Bungay people were not too interested in who managed the Common as long as they continued to enjoy access they had always had to it. As they saw it, only taking it for building land could prevent that — but that was precisely the plan put forward in 1938.

In July of that year East Suffolk County Council's north area joint planning committee wrote to the Common Owners asking that The Hards be scheduled as a public open space. The Owners' reaction was to object immediately to the idea, and the Clerk, Mr. R. H. Sprake, told the planning committee in a letter that The Hards was a valuable building site. There were buildings there which may need to be extended, "and it may be considered necessary to erect a bailiff's cottage."

On July 27th the reeves progressed their opposition by recommending that most of The Hards be zoned for building land. Their idea was that the east end, from the railway to the Urban District Council's pumping station enclosure, should be earmarked for development at eight houses to the acre, and that the middle of The Hards, up to the east end of the enclosure, be zoned for four houses to the acre.

It would have meant 450 homes being built there, though the reeves' plan was that the rest of the Hards should be retained as private open space.

But the Urban District Council, with public opinion behind it, was quick to condemn the idea. It told the planning committee that "the public has had access to the Common on foot and has wandered over it from time immemorial." And it passed a resolution to this effect:

That the council, as representing the general public, and as part owner of Outney Common, is strongly of the opinion that the zoning of the Common as open space, as recommended by the north area joint planning committee, be approved, and that its representatives be instructed to vote in favour of this at the proposed meeting of the

29. A train in Bungay Station, about to cross the bridge beside what was a popular paddling place in the River Waveney on the Common, where the play area is now. On hot summer days the spot was crowded with families. The railway bridge has now been replaced by a bridge carrying the A143 Bungay bypass over the river.

30. One of the former characters of Outney Common – bailiff Broomy Baldry with one of his horses.

Common Owners; and that the council be associated with any appeal which may be made to the Common Reeves.

The Owners' annual meeting on November 28th, 1938, was expected to make a firm decision, and was awaited eagerly or apprehensively, depending on the individual's view. County planning officers were there, and told the Owners that if 15 acres of land adjoining the railway were zoned for factory development, about 450 houses could be erected on the Common under the reeves' recommendation.

After some debate Mrs. Bowerbank proposed the Common be left as an open space for ten years, and this was seconded by Mr. Ronald Wightman, chairman of the Urban District Council, who was there as its representative. Mr. Charles Marston countered this with an amendment that the Owners carry on with the reeves' recommendation for development.

And so to the voting. Owners voted according to the number of goings they owned and so 300 were available. The result was very close: 119 votes were recorded for keeping the Common as an open space, and 123 in favour of the Reeves' housing plan.

But with 58 votes not recorded because Owners were absent, it was inconclusive, and the meeting decided to refer the issue back to the reeves to see if any amicable agreement could be reached.

The Common as we know it today was still safe — and maybe that owes something to the outbreak of the Second World War. No Common Owners meeting was held in 1939, presumably because of the war clouds over Europe, and discussion in 1940 and 1941 concerned an application for rent concessions because of the loss of 16 weeks feed through frost and foot-and-mouth disease (the Owners declined to make any concession), and the problem of goings being overlet during the emergency. The Owners also drew up an agreement with Harry Pointer, of Norwich, in October, 1942, allowing him to take gravel from the Common for use in building aerodromes, including the one at nearby Flixton.

The war also meant military activities returned to the Common, and the problem of protecting the town's water supply from pollution was discussed between the Ministry of Health and the US Staff Officers. But after a break of six years the question of the future of the Common did finally emerge again in April, 1944, and the debate took a new turn, with the Urban District Council asking the Owners if it could buy or lease the whole of The Hards, to enable the town's water supply to be extended and to give it further protection from pollution.

From the Owners' point of view the drawbacks were that if the Hards were sold away from The Lows there would be nowhere to put cattle at times of flooding, and the number of goings would have to be reduced from 300 to 220. Each Owner was written to with details of the proposal and its consequences — the reduction in the number of goings, the fact that £300 maintenance costs would still have to be found even if The Hards were separated from The Lows, booking fees of £25 a year being lost, and so on.

The letter also highlighted the problems facing farming generally at that time:

At a time when the country's programme of ploughing up of upland grass has reduced the pasture acreage in the locality so drastically, the reduction of the grazing available to local farmers and dairymen by another 162 acres is a serious problem...

The National Trust, which owned Common goings (and still does), made it clear it would object strongly to any plans which might have the effect of interfering with the natural beauty of Outney Common " or with the use of that fine open space by the public and commoners. It must be bourne in mind that section 193 of the Law of Property Act, 1925, conferred on the public at large a right of access for air and exercise to commons, and part of this is situated within an urban district. The Trust will not consent to any arrangement likely to prejudice the statutory right."

That view was contained in a letter, dated June 14th, 1944, and signed by the Trust's chief agent, Hubert Smith. It added that if the Urban District Council acquired the Common by compulsory purchase, it would not enclose it without the permission of the Ministry of Agriculture and Fisheries.

The Owners, though, felt the Urban District Council idea worth looking at — but only if the negotiations involved the sale or lease of the whole of the Common, not just The Hards. That was what they agreed, by 12 votes to eight, at a special meeting on June 15th.

But little pertaining to the Common moved at any great speed, it seemed, and the idea lapsed into the background for several years, until more controversy flared up, literally, and brought the management of the Common sharply back into focus once more.

Chapter 12
Fire!

The grass and gorse, made arid by the searing sun,
Was easy victim of the running fire
That sped with fearsome speed o'er dip and mound.
Now Outney was the sudden funeral pyre
And billowing smoke the shroud that closed around
Those Common creatures with nowhere to run.

For a place such as Outney Common, with gorse, furze and fern its predominant vegetation, fire was an ever-present threat. Throughout the centuries, fires large and small have occurred there, and in the times when cattle were pastured on The Hards it was a particular worry to those that owned them. Some records show that at times men were paid to keep watch on the Common for fire.

Paradoxically, in the Great Fire of Bungay of 1688 the Common was not affected, and townsfolk probably took refuge there, dragging along what belongings they could salvage from their burning homes, and erecting makeshift tents to shelter from the wind and cold while they decided what to do.

Interestingly, the Town Trust accounts of 1727 show that John King, Town Reeve that year, paid for men to contain a fire on the Common, and for refreshment for them:

Paid for drink at the fire on the Common, 5s 6d. Paid for more from the Black Horse (probably the former Black Horse pub at Ditchingham), 1s 6d. Paid four men for looking after the fire all night and for four quarters of beer, 5s 4d.

We will presume the cause of this particular outbreak was accidental — often fires were started deliberately by mischievous young people, as in August, 1864. The *Norwich Mercury* of August 6th, 1864, reported:

At about four o'clock on Sunday afternoon the furze growing on the Common was ignited by some boys, and as the grass was very dry the fire spread rapidly, and although several men were employed to extinguish it, between three and four acres of furze were destroyed. The Common Reeves have offered a reward of £5 for the discovery of the offenders, and we have no doubt they will be discovered and punished properly.

Hopefully they were, with people encouraged by the reward, which was a sizeable sum for those days. Rewards were often offered, and sometimes brought success, as was the case following another fire on the Common on July 26th, 1887. Someone who set it alight was caught and convicted, and Inspector George Andrews subsequently applied to be paid the £2 reward offered. But the Common Owners could not agree whether to pay it to him, or a chap called Fred Sampson, who some also felt deserved it. Eventually they decided to give Inspector Andrews £1 10s and Mr. Sampson 10s.

The police certainly had some success in tracking down those who set fire to the Common. On August 7th, 1911, the Common Owners agreed to take proceedings against a lad named Oliver Goldsmith, living with his grandfather in Bungay, for applying a lighted match to the furze that day. This was following information from Sergeant Leftley. When the matter came to court he was given a discharge without fine, but the chairman of the bench, Sir Henry Rider Haggard, told him he had greatly injured the golf course, which was of much value to the town, " all through his wretched carelessness."

Certainly the Common Owners were keen to see those who set fire to the Common punished for their actions, to deter others from doing the same — which made the events of the hot summer of 1959 all the more dramatic and remarkable.

Peter Sprake, Clerk to the Common Owners, deliberately set fire to the gorse on the Common in June and July that year. It was tinder dry and the flames spread rapidly, blackening several acres of grass and gorse in an area just atop the first rise, to the right of the main track.

News, like the blaze, spread like wildfire through the town, and excited children dashed to the Common to watch. The flames may have been spectacular, but there were also sickening sights. Some of those children and teenagers, now adults, speak of the horrible memories of seeing rabbits running from the flames with their fur alight and squeaking in pain.

The fire, and particularly the actions of Mr. Sprake, caused a furore in Bungay, the intensity of which could not have been predicted.

A petition was raised which quickly attracted over 1000 names, and was presented to the Urban District Council. Its members shared the anger and indignation of the townspeople, many of whom attended its meeting on July 17th at which the controversy was debated. The unprecedented weight of feeling against Mr. Sprake's action can be gauged by the fact that the final tally of names on the petition was 7834, 453 members of two print unions signed others (Clay's factory was right alongside the Common, remember), and letters of protest were received from — among others — the golf club, Richard Clay Ltd, and the local Oddfellows Lodge.

The petitioners spoke in strong terms — " A scandalous act of vandalism" and " wanton destruction of the Common" were just some of the phrases used. And Mr. Ron Duhy was equally forceful in speaking at the Urban District Council meeting:

The responsibility for the state in which we find our Common today, a smouldering ruin, lies squarely on the shoulders of one man, whose irresponsible action at the height of the longest drought in the area for years not only destroyed the beauty of the Common, but placed in very grave jeopardy the water supply of the entire town and surrounding districts.

He has shown by his attitude that he is not a fit person to have control of an area in respect of which both public and individual rights and privileges are intermingled.

Mr. W. R. Carr said the matter was an absolute disgrace, and he had never seen the town up in arms so much about anything.

The Urban District Council Clerk, Mr. John Gibbs, tried to put the issue into perspective, reporting that Mr. Sprake had said it had been the intention for the past three years to clear the gorse on the

Common, in order to provide additional feed for cattle (cattle still grazed on the Hards at that time) and to reduce the rabbit population. The fires were controlled, and although the fire brigades were called, he did not think they were needed.

But the meeting was in no mood for conciliation on the issue. The council agreed to send a letter to the chairman of the Common Owners, Mr. Nicolas Bazille de Corbin, calling for Mr. Sprake to be sacked as their Clerk. It also called for steps to be taken to consider bringing the administration of the Common under the control of the Urban District Council, and passed a strongly worded resolution:

This council views with grave concern the action of the Clerk to the Common Reeves in firing the gorse and grass on Outney Common, thereby causing unnecessary suffering to, and destruction of, wildlife and game birds, danger to the council's and other property in the vicinity, and complete disfigurement, for this summer at least, of the town's greatest amenity and attraction for visitors, and asks for assurance that no such action will be taken in future without full consultation and agreement of all parties concerned.

Copies of the resolution were sent to the Reeves, the Ministry of Agriculture, the RSPCA, the National Trust, and the golf club, but the reeves were certainly not contrite. After meeting representatives of the Urban District Council on July 27th, they issued their own statement:

We have carefully examined the evidence, and have gone into the charges made against our Clerk, Peter F. Sprake. We very much regret the Urban District Council action in requesting the dismissal of our Clerk, who is an employee of the Common Owners and does not come under the jurisdiction of the council.

We consider that the council's and other persons' charges against Mr. Sprake are grossly exaggerated and unfounded, particularly as only two fires were started by him, and in our opinion were for the benefit of the Common.

We consider the Council should make a public apology to Mr. Sprake.

Fire!

With regard to the request that steps be considered to bring the administration of Outney Common under the control of the Council, this is a matter which can only be considered at a meeting of the Common Owners. It will be put on the agenda for the next meeting.

Mr. de Bazille Corbin signed the statement, which the Council duly discussed in committee, and then issued another statement of its own, making it clear it had no intention of apologising:

This Council disagrees with the statement made by the Common Reeves, and still considers the Clerk to the Common owners made an error of judgement in lighting any fires on the Common during a prolonged drought. This Council is therefore not disposed to issue any apology. It is desired that the Common owners be asked to meet representatives of this Council at an early date to discuss this and other problems with a view to reaching a solution to the benefit of all concerned.

The Owners got round to considering the issue of the administration of the Common on September 16th that year, and their response probably came as a surprise to the Council, and the people of Bungay; they decided to call for further talks with the Council on the idea of leasing part of the Hards to it, though as with some other important decisions taken by the Owners over the years, the voting was close — 107 all, after a proposal that the Council should have no control at all was countered by an amendment, proposed by Mr. Neville Coe (representing the Town Trust) that talks on leasing should take place.

Meanwhile the Owners agreed to re-seed up to 15 acres of Common previously covered by gorse destroyed in the fires. Gorse has never grown there since for the most part, and most of the area affected is now the 18th fairway of the golf course.

In the negotiations over leasing, it seems the calls by the Council for Mr. Sprake's resignation and the Owners' call for a public apology to him were forgotten.

But the episode did lead to the Council leasing the whole of The Hards (140 acres) from the Owners, leaving them to manage just the Lows, and from that time, except in emergencies, no cattle grazed on

The Hards. The agreement also took in the Little Common and a small piece of The Lows used for bathing — the spot known as Sandy. Both sides agreed to the lease (the Owners voting was 271 for the idea and only two against), and when the Urban District Council received the news at its meeting in December, 1959, Mr. Duhy praised the co-operation the Council had had from the Common Owners and their chairman and Clerk.

A 21-year lease was envisaged, reviewable each seven years, and members were delighted at the news, though Mr. Herbert Whyte sounded a note of caution. He observed that the agreement did not mean the public could go and take away pieces of turf and suchlike — there would still be regulations, just as there were for all public open spaces.

The lease began on May 2nd, 1960, and the Council took on its new responsibility eagerly, quickly drawing up conditions governing The Hards. Generally the arrangements met with the approval of Bungay people — it made them feel that The Hards at least were effectively theirs.

The Urban District Council bylaws for the regulation of the Common came into effect on August 1st, 1961. The maximum fine for offending them was £2. By and large the rules were routine, although, rather quaintly, they included:

" A person shall not, on the grounds, beat, shake, sweep, brush or cleanse any carpet, drugget, rug or mat, or any other fabric retaining dust or dirt," or " hang, spread or deposit any linen or any other fabric for drying or bleaching, otherwise than in the bathing enclosure."

Chapter 13
Commons Registration — Who Owns Outney?

The law lock up the man or woman
Who steals the goose from off the common,
But lets the greater villain loose
Who steals the common from the goose.

From Sir Charles Petre's *Scenes of Edwardian Life.*

In the early 1960s, the Government decided to grasp a large and painful nettle when it resolved to tackle one of the great vague areas of land ownership in England — common land. It was certainly not a problem peculiar to Bungay. Throughout the country thousands of parcels of land were claimed locally to be common land, town or village greens, or waste land, with people in various parishes involved claiming they belonged to the people of the parish, and not to any individual or group.

Many had been the subject of various disputes down the centuries, in modern times they complicated planning applications, and often caused local controversy. The Government decided it was time to try to regularise and simplify the question of ownership.

Its deliberations eventually culminated in the passing of the Commons Registration Act of 1965. This required all commons and greens to be registered by the parishes involved, and it brought to a head the centuries old Bungay debate — who owns Bungay Common?

Considering the fact that it was a subject that had been debated so often, the local re-action to the news was somewhat slow. Indeed, it was only when one of the inhabitants, Leslie Colls, challenged the Common Owners on the matter of shooting rights on the Common for the Bungay Wildfowl Club, that thoughts were turned to it in earnest.

Mr Colls claimed letting the rights was illegal, and letting The Hards to the Urban District Council was also illegal, as was putting up enclosure fences on The Lows. In short, his view was that nothing should be done on the Common to interfere with what he felt were the rights of the people of Bungay to use it freely.

The Owners, at their meeting on October 15th, 1965, were advised by the Clerk that it was essential they established once and for all their rights on these matters. And when they contacted the Urban District Council to discuss the matter as far as the shooting rights on The Hards were concerned, it alerted the council to the new situation.

Clearly, the Council also saw it as an opportunity to establish once and for all that the Common was a common in the historically accepted sense of the word — land for the common use of all its inhabitants. The preliminary reply to the Owners was that the council was not satisfied that the Owners in fact owned the freehold.

Nevertheless, the Common Owners agreed to draw up a lease with the wildfowl club — and the first battle lines were drawn on the issue that was to run for 14 years before reaching a climax.

The Act itself was not mentioned in the Common Owners minute book until April 19th, 1966. Even then it was decidedly brief: "Commons Registration Act, 1965: the Clerk was instructed to apply for exemption under the Commons Registration Act, 1965," it said. The Urban District Council at the same time agreed to apply for Outney Common to be registered as a common under the Act.

The Urban District Council had two main options as far as the Act was concerned — to register Outney Common as a common, a move which would directly challenge the Owners' ownership of it, or to register the Common as a town green. That was a course which would have had much more chance of succeeding, and would have protected the rights of Bungay people to use it for air and exercise, and the various sporting and recreational activities that went on there.

The Urban District Council Clerk at the time was John Gibbs — also an Outney Common trustee for the Owners. It meant that he was in a very delicate position on the negotiations on the registration issue, but he trod a careful and fair course. He emphasised to members that the town green option was the best chance of success, and that the Owners had compelling evidence to back their decision to apply for exemption under the Act.

As far back as 1953, in fact, following a request from a member at the time, Mr. Guy L'Estrange, Mr. Gibbs had thoroughly investigated the ownership issue, and tabled a 14-page report to members in January, 1954, on his findings. His advice then was that the evidence of ownership was compelling, and his view had not changed in 1966.

That 1953 report included details of the sale of commonages — to Henry Atkinson on April 29th, 1769, and to the Duke of Norfolk on September 11th, 1804. In the case of Mr. Atkinson, the commonage was part of a property in St. Mary's Street, and a covenant in the deed gave him "at all times during the said term of 1000 years peacefully and quietly to have, hold, use, occupy, possess and enjoy the said commonage upon the said common called Outney, and all other right, title of commonage or depasturage above mentioned without any lot, suit, trouble, hindrance, denyal, molestation, eviction, interruption or disturbance."

The report also included details of the annual town meeting of 1811, showing that Owners paid less for gravel than non-owners, of the Dr. Beard case, and an extract from Kelly's Directory of 1908 which referred to the management of the Common being undertaken by Common Reeves elected by the Owners.

The rating valuation list of 1908 for the parish of St. Mary's was also included. It showed the Owners of goings, the number they held and the rates they paid for them. The executors of the estate of William Hartcup held most goings, 44, at that time. (The Common continued to be rated until all agricultural land was de-rated under the Ratings and Valuation Act of 1925).

Correspondence relating to the acquisition by the Urban District Council of land on the Common for the waterworks was another element of his report. One letter from the Ministry of Agriculture said that it was "insufficiently informed with regard to the various interests existing on the Common, and it is observed that the ownership of the soil is apparently disputed." The Town Clerk's reply, dated January 19th, 1923, has been quoted in a previous chapter.

The report also noted that the Urban District Council itself bought two goings from Harry Rumsby in January, 1924 (the particular goings involved originally belonged to The Chequers Inn in Bridge Street).

The challenge by Mr. Cecil Clay to the move by the Common Owners to close the Common and make a charge for entry to events on a certain number of days a year was also covered in Mr. Gibb's researches at that time, and he emphasised Sir Lawrence Chubb's statement at the time " that until the passing of the Law of Property Act of 1925 the public had no right to wander over the Common at all."

All this backed up Mr. Gibbs' advice to the Urban District Council in 1966, but the finance and general purposes committee passed a resolution (on January 14th that year) by six votes to five that it did not consider proof of ownership had been shown, and agreed Outney should be registered as a common under the 1965 Act — not to seek to register it as a town green.

The great Common Debate was under way, and later that year the Urban District Council put in train steps to terminate its lease of The Hards from the Owners, with Mr. George Young saying it was " entirely wrong" to enter into an agreement with a body that was suspect.

Mr. Ron Duhy said the ratepayers had called for the lease originally and it would be a retrograde step to end it. Initially the Council was divided, 7-7, when the idea was voted on and chairman Mr Donald Trafford decided to refer the matter back to the committee rather than use his casting vote on such a sensitive issue.

Eventually, though, it was decided to end the lease, and that happened on April 30th, 1967, ostensibly because an agreement could not be reached on a revised rent at the seven-year review. Tacitly, though, it indicated the Council was backing Mr Young's argument that if it was leasing part of the land which was the subject of an application to register it as a common, it could seriously jeopardise the main pillar of their argument — that the Common Owners were not, in fact, legal owners of the land.

The Urban District Council agreed to give up the bathing enclosure at Sandy and re-instate land there, but to continue to maintain the lavatories and equipment at the playground near the golf clubhouse.

The Owners, equally sensitive to every move now, put it on record that they claimed the freehold to the playground land, but would not charge a rent for it.

The zealous Mr. Colls, meanwhile, was ensuring that the issue was kept in the public spotlight. He freely admitted that it was he who had been cutting wires dividing enclosures on The Lows, claiming that the Common Owners did not recognise certain " rights" which he said existed before 1929, and said further wire cutting would occur if those rights were placed in jeopardy.

Eventually, in June, 1967, he landed up in court, charged with carrying a loaded shotgun in a public place, as the result of a dramatic incident at a meeting of the Lowestoft Invaders Motor Cycle Club on the Common on April 29th. He denied the charge, but was convicted, and fined £5.

Briefly, at the meeting attended by about 3000 people, gate steward John Rackham saw Colls, with a shotgun under his arm, cutting the fence near the entrance with a pair of wire cutters. But the hearing gave Colls, himself a Common Owner, another platform to air his views.

He told the court that he had been approached by many ratepayers in Bungay who were dissatisfied with the way the Common was being run by the Reeves, and the suggestions for selling parts of the rights. He had protested at Common Owners meetings that they were doing wrong, and had told the motor cycle club that if it altered the admission notices to " please subscribe" it would have been all right.

He claimed his gun was not loaded. He cut a section of 15 yards of fence, and many people had complimented him on his action.

The *Beccles and Bungay Journal,* in a report on the case at Bungay Magistrates Court, said Colls told the bench: " I told people they could come through and not pay if they wished, or make a voluntary subscription to the Invaders."

People were being deprived of their right to walk across the Common, he claimed.

Michael Harvey, who prosecuted the case, described Colls as "waving the banner for the local populace." Colls' own solicitor, Mr Michael Orr, said his client was acting in good faith. He was representing several people in Bungay, and was genuinely interested in preserving public rights on the Common.

Later Mr Colls gave the Owners an undertaking not to interfere with the Invaders' meeting on July 16th, nor to incite any members of his organisation to do so. He had formed the Colls Organisation, and at a meeting between it, the Common Reeves and the Urban District Council on October 9th, 1967, his solicitor put forward a suggestion for the joint management of the Common involving the Owners and the Urban District Council, under the Common Act of 1899.

It was an ambitious scheme, the central point of which was that all three organisations should declare that the whole of Outney Common was a common under section 193 of the Law of Property Act of 1925 and the Common Registration Act of 1965. Both identified common land as being that giving all inhabitants common use of it.

The scheme proposed that the Common Reeves should be trustees for the Owners of all the goings, and that a committee of management should be drawn up with full powers to regulate and manage it. The committee would comprise two members each from the Urban District Council and Common Reeves, and one each from Bungay Gun Club, the Cherry Tree Angling Club and the local education authority.

No future sale of any part of the Common would be allowed, and the freehold of the Common would be vested in the Urban District Council as custodian trustee, subject to the existing rights of grazing. The proposals envisaged that "the Common shall be held in trust for the use of the inhabitants of Bungay and the neighbourhood without distinction and shall, subject to the rights of pasturage, be used for all forms of recreation and leisure time occupation in accordance with the rules and by-laws laid down by the committee of management, to be approved and enforced by the Urban District Council."

The 14 points in the proposed declaration also envisaged all inhabitants aged 18 and over having the right to attend and vote at the annual meeting of the management committee. Under it, the Urban District Council would have the power to raise a local rate for the running of the Common.

But the Common Owners were not impressed, and most were against the idea. Their advisor, Mr. John Sprake, said while he wanted to see the arguments surrounding the Common resolved, neither the Urban District Council nor the Colls Organisation could offer anything in return for the Owners surrendering certain rights.

When all this was reported to the Owners, they decided to take no action.

Meanwhile research activity by both sides began to hot up. Solicitors searched old minute books, checked old deeds and perused other legal documents in an effort to find firm evidence for their respective cases. Over the ensuing few years the history of the ownership of the Common was studied as never before.

But it was not only the Common Owners and the Urban District Council who were taking notice. There were other bodies which felt, just to be on the safe side, they should stake a claim to the Common and then look more thoroughly into where they stood. Denton Parish Council put in an application for the registration of rights of common under the new Act in June, 1968, and Barclay's Bank followed suit. But both later withdrew their claims, Denton at the persuasion of the Common Owners. Others followed the same course.

It was on June 27th, 1968, that the Common Owners finally formally put in their application to be registered as owners of

Outney Common. It was signed by the three trustees, Mr. Cecil Warnes, Mr. Reggie Reynolds and Mr. John Gibbs (who a year previously retired as Urban District Council Clerk). The Urban District Council put in an application that the Common should be registered as common land under the Act — and the Common Owners duly objected to this on September 21st, 1970.

In December that year the Urban District Council put in its objection (numbered 113) to the Common Owners being registered as owners.

So the two main protagonists had made their positions clear. But the Urban District Council's failure to apply for the Common to be registered as a town green, either as well as, or in addition to, the application for it to be registered as a common, was to prove a vital omission. The fact that it was accepted that Bungay people had always had access to the Common, and engaged in sports and pastimes there, would probably have been sufficient to make that registration stick, and thus preserve those " air and exercise" rights.

In May, 1970, Mr Young, a long-standing campaigner for the rights of townspeople on the Common, claimed at a Council Finance and General Purposes Committee meeting that he was shocked that " through ignorance or some other human error" the town green application had not been registered.

Town Clerk Mr. Desmond Scarle explained that even if the council's application under the Act were to be successful, it would still not prove right of access to the Common for the inhabitants of Bungay. The application in 1967 (before he was appointed) was for the Common to be registered as common land — land over which there were common rights. But it could still be owned freehold by one or more people. Common rights would take in fishing and grazing, but not the right of access to fresh air and exercise, he said.

Those rights would have been obtained it if was registered as a town green, but it was then too late for that.

It was gloomy news for members, but they nevertheless agreed to engage solicitors to advise them on the question of registering the

Common, and to prepare a case for submission to a Commons Commissioner if necessary.

The meeting was evidence that at the time the Urban District Council was having difficulty establishing any firm ownership, though it had been trying for some time. In a letter to Suffolk County Council in January, 1967, it admitted it was impossible to identify the Council's ⅔₀₀ of the Common (it owned two goings), and so could not proceed with registration of ownership. And six months later the East Anglian Water Company (by then responsible for Bungay's waterworks) told the Council it could not register the whole of the Common as common land, because it had granted the company uninterrupted right of way to the pumping station.

It is interesting that while the whole question of ownership of the Common was being debated, the Owners continued to negotiate the sale of part of it. In July, 1967, they agreed to offer the " three Cornered Piece" (an area on the extreme east side of The Lows) to Mr. Tony Hancy for £150 — a sale approved in December that year, though a number of goings owners were against it.

In notes compiled by the Urban District Council solicitors a few years later as they prepared the case for registration, they referred to the sale of gravel for local airfields, part of the Little Common to Clays, and the land to Mr. Hancy, and observed:

The general re-action of the inhabitants to these sales has been one of puzzled fury. In the case of the extraction of gravel, everybody appreciated that it was for the national need, and so it was not challenged. When it came to the sale to Clays, this was obviously a local need and presumably for this reason again was not challenged. However, in the case of the sale to Hancy, this appears to be nothing more nor less than an exercise by the Common Reeves to attempt to establish their right to sell land, and was opposed by a number of goings owners, but went through on a majority.

The general business of the Common continued of course. With the enclosures policy (dividing the Lows into 11 fenced sections and letting each of them) now well established there were just four hirers

— Miss Skinner, Mr. Miles, Mr. John Utting and Mr. Cook — who hired a total of 202 acres at a total rent, including bailiff's wages, of £1460.

Activity continued behind the scenes. In 1970 Mr. Ian Gosling, on behalf of Bungay Cherry Tree Angling Club (based at the Cherry Tree pub which was in Outney Road) put in an application to register rights of access to the Common for fishing. Mr. Edward Buck's application went further — he wanted "rights of shooting, fishing and exercise over the whole of the land" which comprised the Common.

Meanwhile the Owners and the Urban District Council considered compromises in a bid to avoid an expensive legal battle. On March 6th, 1970, Mr. John Sprake, for the Owners, suggested they might seek an out-of-court settlement, and concede to the Urban District Council the right of air and exercise. The Owners decided to take no action on the idea.

Six months later the Urban District Council solicitors made an unofficial approach, saying the Council would agree not to dispute the ownership if the Owners accepted that the Common was governed by the 1925 Act and agreed to apply for a scheme to regulate it.

The Owners view on this was that the Council could provide little evidence to bear out its claim. Mr. Sprake advised them that if they were co-owners they would not be subject to any rights at all, and the reeves and trustees they represented would be devaluing the holding if they agreed to any compromise.

Stalemate again. The Urban District Council, as part of its programme of gathering evidence, appealed to Bungay's inhabitants whose memories went back beyond 1925 to contact them with evidence of their use, or others' use, of the Common as far back as their memories went. There was also a suggestion by Mr. Tony Hood at the meeting that the Council should canvas all Common Owners on the issue in a bid to persuade a majority to withdraw the registration application.

The appeal to the public brought a good response, and solicitors were kept busy interviewing and compiling statements from 70 people aged between 60 and 90. They talked about poorer people regarding the Common as their second home until the second world war, with needy people gathering furze for their own use up to and even beyond that time. They spoke of the practice of grazing cattle on The Hards free of charge, certainly up to the first world war, although grazing on the Haycroft and The Lows was auctioned each year on the instructions of the Owners.

Evidence was also presented that in 1872 and again in 1912 drinking fountains were erected on the Common by the Town Reeve, benches were also put there for public use, and one Town Reeve, Mr. Alfred Cocks, arranged for the planting of a number of trees there.

All this led to the solicitors writing in optimistic tones to the Council in 1971: "While the ownership of the Common is a very emotive issue, we can only say that there is, on the present evidence, a reasonable chance of establishing either the ownership in the Town Reeves, or alternatively, no owner."

This evidence gleaned from townspeople encouraged the Council to make another approach to the Common Owners with a compromise proposal. This time they suggested that, to save legal costs, the Council take over ownership of the Common, with the Owners continuing to receive rents.

But the Reeves rejected the idea as unacceptable, and also turned down the idea that the Owners convey a strip of land to the Urban District Council, with covenants binding the rest of the Common to prevent further sale of land and minerals.

With another impasse reached, the Reeves took steps to appoint counsel to prepare their case, with a cut-off point approaching after which a public inquiry would be inevitable.

The Urban District Council made yet another move for compromise in January, 1972, again seeking a guarantee of air and exercise for residents, and a restrictive covenant conveyed with an area of purchased land. Again it was rejected, with the Owners being advised that the approach must mean the council had a weak case.

But the Owners were not unanimous in their rejection — though they accepted a proposal by Mr. Homer Young that they fight registration and concede nothing, there was an unsuccessful bid by Mr. Geoffrey Alexander for them to consider compromise.

The die was just about cast. The Urban District Council decided to withold rent for the children's playground until the whole issue was settled, and the Reeves established a legal expenses reserve fund to fight the registration battle — a wise move which the Urban District Council, with hindsight, would have done well to follow.

July 31st, 1973, the deadline for settling the issue without an inquiry, passed without settlement, and the matter of ownership of Outney Common passed into the hands of the Commons Commissioners.

Chapter 14
Protests & Battle Lines

*Now I want to tell you something! Here in Bungay
there's a lot o' nonsense about Common owners. Well
there isn't such a thing as a Common owner. All them
people own is a piece of paper entitling them to feed
two head of stock; and that's from the beginning of May
to the end of October...*

Bungay cowkeeper and hayman Charles Hancy, from
an interview recorded by George Ewart Evans in his
book, *The Days That We Have Seen.*

Charles Hancy, who died in 1993 aged 93, was looking back
to the early days of the century in that interview. But his
comments gave an idea of the views many people held in the
1970s (some still do today) as feelings in the town on the future of
the Common were whipped up.

Independently of the Urban District Council, the people of
Bungay began to make their feelings known on the issue. Mr Buck
had already registered his stake to rights on the Common, and
during 1975 a lobby among the townspeople gained momentum,
led by Margaret Mayne (later Margaret Sheppard), a local
councillor. It culminated, in January, 1976, in a protest march
through the town, with hundreds of Bungay people, armed with
placards, making clear their view — that Outney Common belonged
to the town and its residents, who should always have the right to use
it.

The protesters, 200 or so, chanted as they marched, and some of
the placards carried emotive messages. One, carried by Billy Barber,
81 years old and an ardent defender of common rights, read:
" 1914-18 war — many of my school pals gave their lives for
freedom. The Common was their heritage. Where are the Judases

31. The crowd marching from Outney Common down Outney Road during the demonstration in January, 1976, which was part of the move by the Town Council to get it registered as common land under the 1965 Commons Registration Act.

1914 - 1918
WAR

MANY OF MY SCHOOL PALS GAVE
THEIR LIVES FOR FREEDOM.
THE COMMON WAS THEIR
HERITAGE.

WHERE ARE THE JUDASES
WHO WOULD BETRAY THEM?

IN ORDER TO KNEEL AT
THE SHRINE OF MAMMON.

32. The march and rally in January, 1976, organised by those who believed Outney Common should remain as common land, assembled at the Butter Cross. The placard held by Billy Barber clearly states his view.

who would betray them in order to kneel at the shrine of Mammon?"

At a rally at the Butter Cross Mrs Mayne told the crowd that 550 people had signed a petition supporting the council's move to have the Common registered as a common. It had been presented to the council's solicitors, and more names were coming in. Geoffrey Mayne put the case for the council to administer the Common on behalf of the town.

Mrs Mayne said at the end of the rally: " We would not hope to influence the Commissioners' decision. They will go on the facts, but this shows how strongly Bungay people feel about their Common."

The Common Owners private view on the rally was that 500 people made up only one-tenth of the town's population.

Not everyone in Bungay felt so emotionally about the Common issue as those on that march, however. Some were more concerned about the cost to the ratepayers of taking the case to an inquiry, and shortly after the rally, at the monthly town council meeting, their worries were heightened.

Members heard that the bill for preparing and presenting the case could be as high as £2700, and solicitors emphasised that that figure did not take into account any costs which might be awarded against them by the Commons Commissioner. Town councillor Ronald Seamons said at the time that the dispute over Common rights had been going on since he was a child, when meetings were held in the Market Place.

" For goodness sake let's get this thing wiped up...I am sure that 99 per cent of Bungay people would be quite happy to see this thing squared up one way or the other," he said.

But the Council pressed on, and was represented when, at Ipswich on January 22nd, 1976, legal arguments were heard by Commons Commissioner Mr. C. A. Settle. Some members of the Council, and residents, were there, but were not allowed to give evidence.

Mr Edward Buck was, however. Mr Settle heard his claim to register his rights on the Common. He argued that the rights existed for the ordinary person, and his claim was based largely on the fact that he had fished or shot on the Common for many years.

He was putting an argument that numerous other Bungay people who had used the Common for sport and recreation could have put — but he was the only one prepared to do it.

Mr. Settle, however, dismissed Buck's claim on the grounds that he had no documentary evidence to support it. He said no one using the Common had any right to assume ownership.

The hearing on the Town Council's case was adjourned so Mr. Settle could study documentary evidence and get a clear picture of the arguments. But before doing that, he referred to a High Court case, concerning another common. In that instance, the court had said that even if the land had been registered it did not constitute a common because, as at Bungay, no common right had been registered.

It was a disheartening comment from the Council's point of view, and no doubt one which gave the Common Owners great satisfaction. But the Council was now committed to fighting its corner to the end.

In 1974, under the re-organisation of local government, the Urban District Council had become Bungay Town Council, and it took up the fight. Between this time and 1979, both it and the Common Owners redoubled their efforts to find evidence to support their cases — and both were advised optimistically by their counsel on the possible outcome.

Petty disputes inevitably arose between them. In 1975 the Town Council apparently removed a sign banning parking on the Common, and both the Council and Owners claimed the sign was theirs. It was a symptom of the tension between the two at the time.

One side effect of the whole affair was that it hampered plans for the acquisition of land for the proposed Bungay bypass. Part of the Common adjoining the disused railway line along which the new road would run was needed for the scheme (an area of 4700 square metres in all). The problem was, neither Suffolk nor Norfolk County Councils, both involved in the bypass scheme, were quite sure who to approach with the application to buy it. Reluctantly, they had to decide to wait till after the hearing which would decide that, before taking steps to acquire the land, but they probably did not expect the issue to drag on as long as it did.

The Town Council was advised by its counsel, Robin Campbell, in 1977 that there was no significant prospect of any rights of common on Outney being upheld because no specific right of common had been registered before 1970 — the limit laid down in the 1965 Act. But he did feel the registration of Outney as common land should be confirmed by reason of it being waste land of the manor.

Mr. Campbell went to some lengths, in his advice to the Council, to explain why he felt this was the best line to take at the inquiry. It was also complicated, referring to a number of previous cases on similar subjects, and some long established Parliamentary legislation.

The Book of Reference deposited in 1845 when the railway company wanted to buy land to build the railway across the Common contained a long list of people reputed to be Owners. But the book also stated: "His Grace the Duke of Norfolk, as Lord of several manors..claims to be entitled to the soil of this Common."

But in 1864 the Deed Poll executed between the Great Eastern Railway Company, aimed at extinguishing common rights on the land it took for the line, said that "the said common is not parcel or holden of any Manor and the right to the soil of the said common belongs to the commoners." A committee of those entitled to common rights dealt with the company on the matter of compensation, £500 was agreed, and this was paid, in 1860, to the committee.

The procedure adopted for the transaction was laid down in the Land Clauses Consolidation Act of 1845, and Mr. Campbell's view was that the railway company had been scrupulously following the requirements of the Act which applied "with respect to common lands, the right in the soil of which shall belong to the commoners, rather than those requirements laid down for a more normal case where the right of the soil of the lands subject to rights of common indisputably belonged to the Lord of the Manor."

There was evidence, according to Mr. Campbell, that up to that time the ownership of the soil was disputed between the Duke and the commoners, and that the coming of the railway had brought the dispute to a head. But he was convinced that by 1863 the Duke had dropped his claim to the soil, whether or not in the face of determined assertions by the commoners that acts of ownership on their part over the years, such as putting up fences, selling gravel and furze and taking money for grazing donkeys, had defeated his entitlement.

Certainly that was an argument which counted against the Owners in 1883 when they pleaded in the Divisional Court that they should not be treated as rateable occupiers of the Common. They lost that argument — but nearly 100 years later the fact that they did lose stood them in good stead when their Common Registration Act case came before the inquiry.

The fact that since 1863 Bungay people had used the Common for exercise and recreation, or gathering furze, would be seen by a court as more than mere toleration on the part of the Owners of the soil, in Mr. Campbell's view. And in view of this and other cases he referred to, he told the Council in 1977:

I think there is good reason to believe the council can establish its case that the Common is waste land of the manor not subject to rights of common, and by so doing preserve from extinction the public's right pursuant to section 193 of the 1925 Law of Property Act, or access for air and exercise to the Common as being manorial waste, or as a common...situated within an area which immediately before April 1st, 1974, was a borough or urban district.

The fact that the Owners' Clerk, Mr. Peter Sprake, had said in a letter in July, 1958, that there had been free or unrestricted access available to the public, backed that view, he felt.

Eighteen months later it remained the kingpin of the Council's argument when the inquiry finally opened.

Chapter 15
The Decision & the People's Privilege

The remembrance of it (Bath House) has a way of dwelling with people. If it had not already got a name it had had for centuries, I would have called it Green Acres, for before its windows stretch out over 400 acres of marsh and common and heath, brilliant emerald green acres, owned by no man, common to all.

Lilias Rider Haggard, from her book, *Norfolk Life*.

T he inquiry into the dispute was held in London, opening on January 15th, 1979, before Commons Commissioner Mr. C. A. Settle. What he was hearing was an objection by Mr. Cecil Warnes, Mr. Reggie Reynolds and Mr. John Gibbs into the registration of Outney Common as common land being entered in the Register of Common Land maintained by the former East Suffolk County Council — objection No 62; a similar objection by Mr. John Lusby Taylor — objection No 82; and an objection by the former Bungay Urban District Council (taken up by the successor town council) to the Common Owners being registered as owners — objection No 113.

For six days the arguments for and against were vigorously put, with Mr. Robin Campbell, instructed by Mills and Reeve, leading the Bungay Town Council case, and Mr. John Brookes, instructed by Sprake and Hughes, leading the Common Owners' case.

Much of it was legal and technical. Acts were quoted and re-quoted; waste of the manor, rights of air and exercise, ownership of the soil and other key phrases were carefully examined in legal terms. As to the evidence, it spanned more than three centuries, and many facets of the management and use of the Common over that period.

Although the hearing was open to the public, the fact that it was held in London meant only those directly involved were able to go along. Back in Bungay, life went on as normal as its huge area of recreation, natural beauty and working land came under the microscope.When the arguments were all over and the ribbons finally tied on counsels' papers, Mr. Settle went away to prepare his report. Even for a legal man of such experience, it was a complicated issue to unravel. Indeed, immediately after the hearing, solicitor Miss Louise Tee said in notes to the Town Council:

I think you are well aware that your case was a very difficult one, and indeed the Commissioner had never dealt with a case quite like it.

Mr. Settle's decision was conveyed to the Town Council and the Common Owners in documents dated March 14th, 1979. It covered eight pages.

The report noted that in the 15th, 16th, 17th and 18th centuries the Common was manorial land subject to common grazing rights, but that "the precise nature and origin of those grazing rights is obscure."

It noted that within living memory there had been 150 such rights, known as commonages, which in some cases were sub-divided into goings, with the owner of a going entitled to graze one beast. It said the Common had been managed by the Common Reeves, on behalf of the commoners, who also made charges for gravel taken from the Common, and for the grazing of donkeys.

"As long ago as 1811 the commoners were taking rent and profits from the Common to which they were not entitled by virtue of their commonages," the report said.

It also noted that the inhabitants of Bungay "have always had access to the Common and engaged in sports and pastimes on it. No claim has been made that the Common or any part of it is a Town Green, and the only relevance of this use of the Common is to explain the council's anxiety to preserve the Common as an amenity for its constituents."

Now, commonages were regarded as investments by their owners, "who are concerned with capital appreciation, and the yield which these investments will provide."

The Council urged at the hearing that Mr. Settle should confirm the registration of the Common in the land section of the register on the grounds that it was subject to common rights at the date of registration, and that it was waste land of the manor.

The report said Mr. Brookes conceded that the Common was at one time manorial land, and that it was up to him to prove that the Lord of the Manor had no claim on it at the date of registration. Mr. Settle saw as crucial to the argument the acquisition of a small part of the Common in 1864 by the Great Eastern Railway Company. The transaction was effected by an indenture dated July 8th, 1864, discharging the land acquired from all commonable rights. In addition, a Deed Poll dated November 11th, 1864, vested the land in the railway company free of all commonable rights.

Both documents said the Common was " not parcel or holden to any manor, and the right to the soil of the said Common belongs to the commoners." Mr. Settle said in his view that was evidence that the commoners were the Owners of the soil in 1864. He said negotiations on the building of the railway had begun in 1859, and if the Lord of the Manor, believed to be the Duke of Norfolk, had wanted to claim compensation for his interest in the soil, he had every opportunity to do so.

(Apparently the fact that on September 11th, 1804, the Duke of Norfolk bought two commonages belonging to the King's Head Hotel in Bungay was not available to the inquiry. That indicated that 60 years before the railway transaction the Duke accepted that he had no interest in the soil, other than as a Common owner).

In any event the inquiry report added: " 1864 is a long time ago, and subsequent events disclose that the Common Owners from 1864 to the present day have exercised rights of ownership."

In 1882, in the Queen's Bench division of the High Court, the Common Owners appealed against an assessment to rates on the grounds that they were only exercising their common rights and so were not rateable. The court decided that they were rateable, and though Mr. Settle accepted that that did not necessarily mean they were the owners of the soil, the decision was " consistent with the commoners having at that time disposed of the Lord of the Manor," of whom nothing had been heard since 1707.

The plans for a steeplechase course on the Common in 1888, the erection of a grandstand in 1912 and an agreement in 1923 to close the Common for not more than 12 days a year for racing, were other instances cited of the Common owners making agreements relating to the Common, and Mr. Settle observed that the Urban District Council was party to the closure of the Common, in agreeing that the lands " are not parcel of or holden of any manor, and that there were no rights of common or other rights affecting the land, other than those of the lessees and tenants or rights for 300 beasts."

Mr. Settle also noted that the Common Reeves entered into an agreement in February, 1889, with the Waveney Valley Golf Club, for the construction of golf links on the Common, and since then, rent for the lease had been paid to them.

Other transactions involving the Common Owners and Reeves with the Urban District Council, the Anglo American Oil Company (1922), the GER again (1926) and Harry Pointer (Norwich) Ltd in 1942 were all cited at the hearing, and Mr. Settle said though the inquiry was not concerned about establishing who was the owner of the Common :

....the fact of the matter is that the Common Owners, by their agents and Common Reeves, have been in possession of the land since 1864, even if they were not then the owners. They have dispossessed the true owner in that they have taken rents for the golf links and the race course...they have taken rent from the railway company and the Anglo American Oil Company, and the Urban District Council and Richard Clay and Company Ltd, they have taken the proceeds of the sale of gravel and turf.

In short, the Common Owners and they alone have been in receipt of the rents and profits.

In my view the possession of the Common Owners has been more than adequate to bear any claim to ownership by the Lord of the Manor, and any title he once had has been extinguished.

Mr. Settle added that the land had not been " waste" for nearly a century. " It follows from what I have said that I must refuse to confirm the registration in the land section, and I therefore have no jurisdiction to deal with the question of ownership," he said.

Those words, effectively, spelled the end of Bungay's claim that Outney Common, on which people had enjoyed free access for centuries, belonged to the inhabitants. The decision meant they had no legal right to use it.

Mr. Settle also dealt with the question of whether any common rights still existed on Outney Common. He compared the situation at April 28th, 1921, when 22 commonages — 44 goings — were sold, with the sale particulars prepared by Sprake and Co, saying: " Each commonage represents two goings, or the right of depasturage for two beasts...each commonage comprises $\frac{2}{300}$ equal undivided parts or shares in the Common," with that in 1963.

Then all commoners, apart from one, signed documents stating:

I the undersigned, being the owner of x goings on Outney Common, hereby endorse the action of the Common Reeves in the enclosures they have already made on a trial basis, and now formally and irrevocably consent to the whole of The Lows being fenced and enclosed on a permanent basis, and to the sole letting thereof in future by the Common Reeves.

Said Mr. Settle:

In my view each commoner, by signing a document in this form, abandoned his right to graze a beast on The Lows, or it may be regarded as a release. The release of a right over part of a common operates as a release of the right over the whole common. At the annual general meeting of the commoners held on March 28th, 1963, the chairman stressed the importance of all owners signing the form of consent.

The necessity to obtain the consents of all the commoners supports my view that the individual rights were still subsisting at that date. The object of obtaining the consents was to determine these individual rights, and in my view had that effect.

In fact at that time three owners, Mr. Biles, Miss Kathleen Bowerbank and Mr. F. A. Laws, had refused to sign the consent. Lengthy consultations took place with the Commons Preservation Society and by June, 1963, all but Mr. Laws had signed the forms of consent.

Mr. Settle went on:

I was told at the hearing that the one dissentiant's goings had been acquired by another Common Owner, who had signed a consent. The Bungay Urban District Council signed a consent, and this no doubt accounts for the fact that it did not apply for registration of a right of common.

For this reason I am of the opinion that all rights of common were extinguished in 1963, with one exception. I do not know whether that exception was still outstanding at the date of registration. The town council may consider that in any event it would be an insecure foundation on which to build an appeal.

So an historic chapter in the book of Outney Common closed. But it is worth noting that there was some evidence of goings in property deeds up to very recent times that was not presented at the inquiry, contrary to the popular view that they were all sold away from properties before this century.

In fact, it is known that a property in Beccles Road, built as recently as 1915, had in its deeds the right to graze a cow on a going on the Common. When that property last changed hands, in 1978 — intriguingly, just a few months before the inquiry into the Common registration — that right was still there. No caveat or codicil had been added to the deeds noting that the right had been detached or sold away from the property.

Frustratingly, the deeds have gone missing, so that the precise wording on them relating to the grazing of a cow cannot be checked.

Had that evidence been available to the inquiry, it may well not have altered the Commissioner's decision, of course. His view that all rights of common were extinguished in 1963 following the Owners move towards enclosures would still have stood, no doubt.

No efforts have been made by the owner of the Beccles Road property to claim any grazing right. But it is evidence that even in very recent times such rights were recorded in property deeds, and it may be that where one instance has come to light, there may be deeds of other properties in Bungay which still include such a right, even though it is now obsolete.

Thus Outney Common was not registered under the Commons Registration Act, 1965 — a result which brought great satisfaction to the Owners, and great disappointment to the Town Council, and those residents who had actively campaigned for it to be declared a common on which everyone had rights of use.

The inquiry had decided, in effect, that the Common Owners' position was exactly that — they were the owners of the soil of the Common, free to administer it and control it and who or what went on it. It was what the Owners and Reeves had in fact been doing for the previous 280 years or so.

Frustratingly from the town's point of view, Mr. Settle found that inhabitants of Bungay had always enjoyed free use of the Common, for sport, pastimes, recreation, walking and other activities. That would have been sufficient to register it as a town green — but, as recorded earlier, the Council had decided not to take that course.

It was then, not at the hearing in 1979, that that opportunity, which would have given the people of Bungay some legal rights over those 400 or so green acres, was lost.

The Town Council, already facing crippling legal costs as the price for taking their case to an inquiry, did consider the possibility of an appeal, despite Mr. Settle's comment. But to take it to the Court of Appeal would have been another excessively expensive venture which the ratepayers would have had to pay for.

Notice of an appeal was lodged, but the Town Council decided to get the view of the townspeople. At the annual Town Meeting at the Community Centre on April 25th, 1979, about 90 people were present and their overwhelming view was that an appeal should not go ahead. Only three voted against the motion that carried that proposal. Town Council chairman Mr Ivor Baldwin said the inquiry decision would make no difference to the use of the Common by Bungay people, and with the financial aspect of an appeal hanging heavily over the town, most were only too ready to accept that. It was a matter of cutting the town's losses.

The Common Owners, meanwhile, had always been confident of victory in the dispute, and welcomed the decision at their meeting on May 24th, 1979, when they also heard the Commons Commissioner had awarded costs at the highest scale allowed against the Town Council.

Reaching a final figure for the exact costs took some time. Two years later Owners chairman Mr Nicolas de Bazille Corbin told his members: " At a later date I shall be in a position to report the final net cost to the Owners resulting from the Town Council's rather rash action in trying to register the property as a common under the Act."

Perhaps, in retrospect, some councillors admitted it was rash. Certainly many residents did, though equally as many still felt it had been a fight worth taking on. Whatever their view, each ratepayer had to contribute to the legal bills, which were not finally defined until three years after the hearing.

The total cost to the Common Owners was £18, 605.98. But the Town Council had to pay £13, 372 of that, leaving the Owners with a net bill of £5233.54.

With their own costs to pay as well the Town Council had to find over £25,000 altogether — and the Owners obviously discussed how they might obtain the funds from the Council if they were not forthcoming in a reasonable time. Their minutes of April 30th, 1981, record:

It was decided not to ask the court to put in bailiffs to seize Council property at this stage, but to wait a little longer for settlement. The Owners' solicitors were left to deal with the collection of the award.

It would have been heavy handed action indeed. But the Council bill was eventually settled in the normal way.

At about this time the Owners were in discussion on a lucrative deal in which they would sell gravel from the Common for the construction of Bungay bypass which, with the ownership issue settled, was now going ahead with all speed. In all 85,000 cubic metres of gravel would be needed, and 25,000 cubic metres of peat and topsoil would have to be disposed of. The gravel would be taken from the area near the pond, and it could bring £150,000 into the Owners' coffers, they heard.

It was an inviting prospect. The Town Reeve, Mr. John Franklin, told the Owners at the time that the Town Trust approved of the idea, but also asked " that in the interests of goodwill and civic solidarity the Common Owners give serious consideration to the making of a financial contribution to the town of, say, 20 per cent of the proceeds of the sale, this sum to be used in the interests of the citizens of Bungay."

There is no record of the Common Owners re-action to the idea. In any event, though they decided to go ahead with a planning application in connection with it, a deal was never concluded, and the bypass contractors got their gravel from another site almost next door to the Common.

Its shape, therefore, remained unchanged. The final land deal to take place saw the final piece of the Little Common, a small area at the top of Outney Road left when Clay's built its warehouse, sold to Suffolk County Council in 1982 for a total of £9000.

In the wake of the decision on ownership, efforts were made to have further public footpaths declared over the Common. Two public meetings were held in Bungay on the issue, on September 18th and 21st, 1979, but the Owners declared their opposition to any such moves, and no new footpaths were declared. The only public footpath over the Common is the one from the public footbridge over the bypass, past the pond and over the Lows to Ditchingham.

But in 1995 the Owners did encourage walkers to walk the river banks around the Common by putting in new stiles, and a new wooden bridge over a dyke at the bottom of the Common, all marked with footpath waymarkers.

It is worth noting that in the run-up to the inquiry Mr. Ian Gosling registered the bed of the River Waveney around the Common under the Act in an effort to protect fishing rights. An inquiry into that was held by Commons Commissioner Mr. L. T. Morris at Ipswich on February 26th, 1980.

Mr. Gosling was represented, but made no claim to ownership, and as a result, on May 26th, 1981, the Common Owners were declared as owners of the bed of the river, too.

Chapter 16
Flora & Fauna

On certain still, hot nights in summer, when the wind is in the south and the moon rises late, the eel-babbers come to the Common side of the river which runs at the foot of my garden...

Very quiet it is then. Sandpiper, plover and strong flighting swans are gone with the tumult of spring. The voice of the frog, and the continuous quivering drum of the nesting snipe have fallen silent. Later on the owls will begin their autumn chorus, but now only the chatter and creak of the reed bunting sounds through the warm dark.

Lilias Rider Haggard, in her preface to *I Walked by Night*, the story of the King of the Norfolk Poachers, which she edited.

T hat beautifully descriptive prose catches well the atmosphere of Outney Common, not only at the time that it was written, but as it is today. And, despite all the controversy, all the argument, all the campaigning and all the worry, it is an amenity which is just as accessible to the people of Bungay as it was then.

That was a promise made, almost as soon as the ink was dry on the inquiry decision documents, by the Common owners' chairman at the time, Nicolas de Bazille Corbin. It is recorded in the Owners' minute book that when Town Council hairman Mr Ivor Baldwin asked if future access to the Common would continue now that the Owners had been awarded legal ownership, "the chairman assured him, on behalf of the Owners, that there was no intention to alter the present situation or the privileges afforded to the public."

It is a privilege they are continuing to enjoy, with few problems or complaints either way, in large numbers — perhaps in greater numbers than at any time in its history.

The Bungay and Waveney Valley Golf Club went through a low point in the 1950s but has grown rapidly since then. It opened a splendid new clubhouse in 1985, and currently has a membership of 600 and a waiting list. The course over The Hards is still one of the most picturesque in the Eastern Counties, and there are few days when its fairways and greens are not busy.

In some areas the course is cramped, however, and in 1994 the club asked the Owners if it could be extended by 25 acres, using land towards the bottom of the Hards, to make it safer for players and public alike.

Inevitably the request brought reaction from some residents against the idea, and after some debate, both public and private, the Owners voted narrowly (a two-thirds majority was needed) against the extension.

Two years later, though, an amended scheme for an extension covering 11 acres was backed by the Owners. It now remains to be seen whether the Broads Authority allow it.

Golf is now the only organised sport taking place on the Common — but many are the people who use it for walking and exercising their dogs, enjoying " the right of air and exercise" referred to so often. Families enjoy informal sport, rounders, cricket, football and fishing, flying kites, swimming in the river at Sandy, boating there and generally taking advantage of the wide open spaces. It is a marvellous place for a walk.

Cattle still graze The Lows as they have done for centuries. Only the breeds have changed, with Jerseys the most common now. Still the Common is divided into 300 goings for ownership purposes, owned by varying numbers of people. But communal grazing has disappeared, and the Lows are now divided into 11 enclosures which are let annually. Currently just two farmers, Mr. John Utting, of Mettingham, and Mr. Graham Crickmore, of Bungay, hire them.

The change from open grazing to this system was triggered during the 1950s by the introduction of testing for cattle against tuberculosis and brucellosis. The Owners agreed that, as from May, 1955, only attested stock would be allowed on the Common, and two years later, four enclosures were set up as an experiment. The following year, 1958, a reserve of £5 an acre was set for the enclosures, with the hirers being responsible for cutting the thistles and nettles at least once before they flowered. Only one horse was allowed per ten acres. The remaining 222 goings were let for communal grazing at 70s a going for the first 150.

By this time, cattle were only allowed on the Hards in times of flood. The system of enclosures was extended over the years and by 1963, when all goings owners gave up their right to communal grazing, as already explained, there were nine.

As well as preventing the spread of disease, the enclosure system as it operates today (with 11 enclosures) is more convenient for the Owners and the hirers, and produces greater income. Hirers can have as many cattle on the Common as they wish, can make silage of part of it, and the pasture is generally cared for a lot better than it was previously, when grazing had become very poor. Now, the Lows are considered as good as any marshes in Norfolk or Suffolk.

The practice of keeping the Common free of cattle and other animals during the winter, set up around 290 years ago, still holds good today, though the dates vary. They are taken off during November, and return there in April, depending on the conditions.

The landscape of the Hards has varied over the years. Pictures of it in the 1920s and 1930s show it as rather bare, broken only by the gorse, and with the wooded Bath Hills backdrop, with its variety of deciduous trees, providing much of its beauty.

Edgar Watts Ltd, maker of willow clefts for the manufacture of cricket bats — used by many of the world's top batsmen — had an arrangement with the Owners to grow willow trees there, and lines of them became a familiar feature along the bank of the Waveney and in other areas. In 1969, when the Owners were considering charging the company more for the privilege, Miss Kathleen Bowerbank did a count, and reported that there were 1755 willows, with more to count. Almost all have now been felled, though the company ceased to make willow clefts in 1990, the trade being continued by some former employees.

Unlike the willows, numerous young oaks and silver birch trees on the Common are self-sown, and have become part of the landscape in recent years, and part of its beauty. Now though, a programme of grubbing out the smaller ones has taken place, reducing their numbers, but copses of young trees are still there to provide variety, and hazards on the golf course, where conifers also abound.

The days are long since gone when the various natural products of Outney Common were sold to Bungay people — furze, silt, gravel, stones and the like. But there is one product that townspeople still help themselves to free — blackberries.

Brambles cover many parts of The Hards, and in late summer and autumn people can be seen gathering their plentiful harvest in baskets and bags — every year many hundreds of pounds of the juicy black fruit find their way from there into pies, jams and jellies in local homes.

Two varieties of blackberry abound — the more common, oval-leafed one, and an interesting one with pear-shaped leaves, known as the cut-leaved, or American blackberry.

Naturalist Mr. Ted Ellis was fascinated by it. He told Miss Bowerbank in a letter that its origin was unknown, "but I am fairly sure that it arose as a mutant from the very common Rubus ulmifolius. I found it in great abundance on Outney Common in 1973, which astonished me, as it is found only rarely as a garden escape. It was parasitised by the rust-fungus which commonly attacks several of our wild brambles. I know of no other site in Britain where it is present in such large numbers."

Because of its "American" label, the thought arose that it may have been introduced to the Common by the Americans stationed at Bungay during the Second World War, but there appears to be no substance to that theory. However it arrived, it provides the most succulent fruit.

Brambles are just one of the many different flora and fauna that make the Common such a fascinating place for botanists and naturalists. A survey carried out in 1986 by the Suffolk Wildlife

Trust's habitat team logged 250 different species, and said the list was unlikely to be exhaustive. It said in its report:

This extensive area of acid grassland represents an uncommon and decreasing habitat in north-east Suffolk. Many sites of a similar nature have been lost, and Outney Common is probably the largest area of its kind east of Wortham Ling, near Diss.

Records of local naturalists are included in the Trust's list of plants, grasses, shrubs and trees. It says they include at least 30 plants uncommon to the area, or which are now rarely found, due to loss of habitat.

The most notable of them is bulbous meadow grass (poa bulbosa), which has one of its biggest inland sites in Britain on the golf course. There are more than 25 species of grass alone on the Common. The Trust's view is that much of Outney Common is of great nature conservation value, and should be managed with that objective in mind. It is a view the Owners are taking heed of at the present time.

There is an abundance of animals and birds on the Common. The song of the skylark is one of the most familiar sounds there, and they can be seen soaring high above the ground. Along with the linnet the skylark is probably the most common bird found there. The heron, with its familiar lazy flight, or standing like a post on the marshes, can also be seen regularly.

Towards dusk, barn owls nesting in the wooded Bath Hills can be spotted hunting their prey, systematically combing the marshes or heathland area and suddenly dropping down to seize an unwary vole or fieldmouse, and then making for home again to feed its young.

Swans are another of the beautiful sights. There are many on the River Waveney there, and those who walk regularly along the banks in the spring can follow the progress of families from nesting time to when the cygnets hatch and take to the water themselves, shepherded proudly by their parents.

Less easy to spot are kingfishers, but their flash of shimmering blue and orange can be seen on occasions in the river bank. And

33. The plaque on Outney Common marking the planting of a copse of trees to celebrate the 25th anniversary of Queen Elizabeth II's accession in 1977.

34. The unchanging scene on The Lows - cattle grazing.

migrating sand martins are regular summer visitors, making their nests in the sandy part of the " cliff" — the side of the quarry dug during the second world war for gravel to build aerodromes.

Other regular visitors to the Common are the cuckoos, easily heard and often seen, perhaps sitting in the top of one of the remaining willows, or maybe chasing another bird whose nest it has planted its eggs in.

Sometimes great-crested grebe spend time on the pond, and can be seen teaching their young to dive. Cormorants have been known to find their way there, perhaps having lost their bearings or coming inland for food. In recent years a steadily growing flock of wild geese has settled on The Lows — wildlife to be found among the many common small finches and other birds for which the Common is home.

Rabbits abound there. Over the years the Common Owners have regularly had to address the problem of controlling them and have tried a variety of methods, including shooting and gassing, but they have never managed to eradicate them — they have always regrouped and multiplied again. Myxamatosis in the 1950s greatly reduced the problem for some years.

The problem of rabbit infestations was discussed by the Owners at their meeting on April 26th, 1976, when they agreed to let the Rabbit Clearance Society shoot the area for a period. Success was limited, and two years later gorse was burned off as a rabbit control exercise, but that brought complaints from the public, and was only marginally successful anyway. Gassing was tried in the 1980s, with better results, but numerous burrows on the Common today are evidence that the rabbit population is still high, and that they are still a problem. Moles also abound, despite efforts over the centuries to control them — men used to be paid as mole-catchers at one time. Other small animals such as voles, fieldmice, weasels and stoats are less of a problem, and the occasional fox is seen.

And of course there are the cattle, grazing on The Lows, just as they have done for hundreds of years — part of the unchanging scene the Common presents in an ever-changing world. But the old

35. An atmospheric scene at dusk on Outney Common with trees and cattle silhouetted, and the Old River in the foreground reflecting the setting sun.

36. The bridge over the former railway line, linking the Little Common with the Common proper. The picture was taken in 1981 shortly before the bridge was demolished.

rule of not grazing the land between December and April still holds good, so the pasture has time to recover for another season.

To allow, as was said in the document of 1707, for that part of nature's eternal cycle, "the springing of the growth of the grass..."

The springing of the green.

Chapter 17
Common Bits & Pieces

The water had come down so quick there had been no time to git all the stock off the Common, and six or seven horses were driven up onto the last bit of high ground sticking up above the flood. They had to go out to them in boats, halter one of the old mares and lead her through behind one of the boats and git the other young 'uns to foller.

George Baldry: *The Rabbitskin Cap.*

The beauty and serenity of Bungay Common is acknowledged — many people and many writers have paid tribute to it over the years. But there are also times when it can take on a sinister, forbidding, even frightening, atmosphere.

George Baldry's observation here shows the dire problems the elements can cause on the marshy Lows. but in *The Rabbitskin Cap* he recounts an even more tragic happening.

He recalled that one afternoon his grandmother, " getting on in years," picked up the bucket yoke as usual to go to milk the cows grazing on the Common. He goes on:

The bounders had strayed — she was a long time a'gittin' them up, and by the time they was milked it was day's end, and a fog with it, thick as a feather bed.

She missed her way among the dykes and wandered all night, not knowing which way to turn, still a-carrying the milk pails, and when dawn came, found herself right over by Bungay. She got home six o'clock time, exhausted — and died two hours later.

It is easy to imagine the panic and fright of the old lady as the fog closed in and she wandered around with the heavy bucket yokes still to carry, stumbling through dykes and gorse as she tried to regain her bearings, only to become further disorientated. And that was someone who knew the Common as well as anyone.

*

Charles Hancy recalls as a ten-year-old going on the Common early one morning to get the cows in for milking in " a proper thick fog" and losing his bearings. He found himself down at the bottom of the Common, having been driving the cows away from home. In the end he had to let them go, and they found their own way home. He told George Ewart Evans, who, in his book *The Days That We have Seen* recorded the story:

I knew that old Common from A to Z, but it was so thick that morning you couldn't see where you were. You'd got to be careful you didn't walk into the river or into the dykes. It's a proper dangerous owd place when it's thick.

*

The Owners took what steps they could to protect the Common from disease. Following an outbreak of the cattle plague, a notice was issued in the town in January, 1877, stating that no stock bought from Norwich Hill (the Norwich cattle market where the Castle Mall shopping complex now is) would be allowed on the Common without being professionally examined (by a veterinary surgeon), or until seven days after they came from the Hill.

*

The newest sporting use for the Common is as a cross-country course. The Bungay Black Dog Running Club has held an annual cross-country race over a 2.8-mile course there since 1990. In 1991 and 1992 it was the venue for an outdoor drama production by the Company of the Imagination as part of the annual Bungay Festival.

*

There are many people still living in Bungay who referred to one area of the Common as The Roman Camp. It was the name local people gave to an earthwork near the Broad Street entrance to the Common, where the bypass roundabout now is. The building of the roundabout destroyed the last remnants of it, but it consisted of portions of the ramparts of a square or rectangular enclosure,

152

37. Peaceful scene on the Common in Edwardian times, with one couple (Mr and Mrs Edwards) fishing, and a family boating.

38. Finches Well, the deepest part of the River Waveney, pictured today as it winds around the Common. A man called Finch is said to have drowned there.

according to archaeologist William Dutt, who studied it. Even by 1905, much of the ramparts would have disappeared with the building of the railway, but at that time the bank on the north side of the enclosure measured 45 yards in length, the west side 72 yards, and the south side 27 yards. They were about 2.5 feet high, and were a favourite play place for local children.

Dutt says, however, that there was nothing to connect them with the Romans, and they may have been the remains of some of the boundaries of the "common fields" of medieval times. He also claims that before the building of the railway, there were four mounds near the entrance to the Common, which may have been barrows — prehistoric grave mounds.

*

Artist Alfred Munnings has already been mentioned. Another eminent person who also took inspiration from Outney Common was Sir Henry Rider Haggard, author of 58 novels, including *King Solomon's Mines* and *She*, as well as numerous other publications and articles.

He lived at Ditchingham House for much of his life, and also spent a lot of time at Ditchingham Lodge, close to the Common on the Norfolk side of the Waveney. The view from Bath Hills across the Common was one of his favourite scenes. When he died in 1925 his daughter, Lilias Rider Haggard, gave the south-east window of St Mary's Church, Ditchingham, in his memory, and that view over the Common to Bungay is one of three scenes associated with Sir Henry's life which can be seen in stained glass as part of the window. The others are the pyramids of the Nile, and his farm in Africa, where several of his novels were set.

*

A third notable figure with links with the Common is the French aristocrat, Francois de Chateaubriand. An emigre living in great poverty in London, he came to Beccles in 1793 at the invitation of Mr Bence, the rector, to decipher some French manuscripts which were among the Camden papers. Introduced to the Rev. Ives and his family he spent some time at their house in the winter of 1793 recovering from a fall from his horse.

He was much taken by their teenage daughter, Charlotte. Some years later, having returned to France, he became part of the King's court and was French Ambassador to Britain for a spell. In his memoirs he fondly recalls his time with the Ives, and Charlotte in particular, and the long walks he enjoyed with her during his convalescing. It is almost certain that some of those walks were on Bungay Common — it was a short step from her home along Nethergate Street.

*

Goings on Outney Common don't come up for sale very often these days. When they do they are sold privately, and the price today is £1000-£1500 a going. One was sold in 1993.

Years ago they tended to be sold by auction — the last time that happened was in 1980, at a sale conducted by estate agents and auctioneers Durrant's at the Fleece Hotel at Bungay on September 11th. Two belonging to the late Mr Charles Rowe were sold on the instructions of his executors, and fetched £1500 — £750 each. Twenty others were sold in five lots on the instructions of the executors of the late Mr Arthur Wright, with prices varying between £2050 and £2600 for five.

The particulars of sale described them as "Twenty equal $\frac{1}{300}$ parts of all the common pasture known as Outney Common." It said deeds described them as "twenty undivided three-hundredth parts of all that common pasture called Outney situate in Bungay, Suffolk...all those ten commonages and rights of depasturing twenty head of stock."

But it also made clear that the rights of individuals to graze was discontinued when the Lows was divided into enclosures.

*

There is a map of the Common, dated 1772, held at the Suffolk Records Office at Lowestoft, prepared by Samuel Lillestone, of Beccles. It shows Finches Well, once one of the popular swimming places on the Common, and thought to have been named after a man who once drowned there. The scale of the map is four chains to the inch, and has the Old River marked, running through the centre of The Lows.

*

When those planning an annual cattle fair at Olland's Farm at Bungay were considering another site for it, the Owners were quick to cut out any thoughts of it being held on the Common. They said in a notice dated April, 1831: "The injustice of so deprecating the property of every poor inhabitant who has hired a going for his cow, to assist him in avoiding parish relief, is manifest to all who are not blinded by self-interest, or indifferent to the appropriation of the property of their neighbours."

It warned that the Owners could take action if steps were taken to hold a cattle fair there. In the event, it did not take place.

*

There has been a bridge over the river from the Common, linking Bungay with Ditchingham, for centuries. In January, 1886, the public called for the bridge, known as the mill bridge because on the Ditchingham side it was near the former water mill which once stood there, to be raised so boats could pass underneath. At the time the Owners decided it could be raised, but at the public's expense, and nothing was done about the idea.

It was not until 1922 that the then Town Reeve, Mr. H. N. Rumsby, erected a unispan bridge there to mark his year of office, and it is still there today.

A new stock bridge had been erected over the Old River on the Common in 1892 for use in case of emergencies. Today there is a footbridge only there, for public use.

*

In 1977 the Common Owners discussed the possibility of marking the Queen's Silver Jubilee in some way, and the planting of a clump of trees was discussed. It was something that the chairman, Mr. de Bazille Corbin, was particularly keen on, but the Owners felt the projected cost of £350 was too much and decided not to go ahead with it. However the chairman, who represented the National

157

Trust (he was its regional agent) on the Owner's body, was not to be outdone, and arranged for the trees to be planted at no cost to the Owners.

Today, they are maturing well on the east side of the Hards, and are marked by a plaque which says: " Outney Common — These trees (Populus Alba and Populus Canescens) were planted in 1977 at the expense of the National Trust and the Countryside Commission to commemorate the silver jubilee of the accession of Queen Elizabeth II. N. de Bazille Corbin, Regional Agent for the National Trust."

*

A stock bailiff was first appointed for the Common in 1897, following the Dr. Beard controversy, and those that held the post in ensuing years tended to be characters, men of the common, in their own right.

The first was George Everett, always known as Friday Everett, who did the job for 17 years, after doing casual work for the Owners from time to time. The work involved looking after the cattle, locking the gates at appropriate times, rescuing cows from dykes, mending fences, cleaning out dykes and seeing that no one offended the regulations.

Alfred Barber took over as bailiff at the start of the first world war, with the thankless task of trying to run the Common and protect the cattle while war manœuvres were taking place. Among other things he had to help sort out the mess when a Zeppelin dropped bombs which missed the Army encampment but slaughtered and injured many cows grazing there.

When he retired in 1931 John (" Broomy") Baldry took on the job, and became a popular figure on the Common, particularly among the youngsters who used to play there. They used to " play him up" to some extent, but he usually took it all in his stride.

As with the other bailiffs Mr. Baldry, who lived close to the Common in Broad Street, had to be able to recognise each of the 300 cattle individually and remember its owner's name, so he could inform them if anything went wrong. Initially he used to cycle round the Common on his work — later he got about in a cart drawn by a white pony, Tom, given to him by Mrs. Steward of Spexhall, whose family was part of Steward and Patterson the brewers. Tom and Broomy retired together, and died within four weeks of each other.

The youngsters, of course, were very good at getting up to mischief. They often used to " borrow" Mr. Baldry's boat, which he used to retrieve cattle which sometimes crossed the river to the Norfolk side, for fun and games, and eventually it disappeared altogether!

Mr. Baldry gave up the job full-time in 1950, but continued to do it part-time for a further 11 years until, in 1961, Mr. R. C. Cook was appointed to the job. By the time Mr. John Crickmore took over 13 years later, in 1974, it had become, because of modern methods, much less onerous than it was in the early years of the century.

Today there is no bailiff as, with just two farmers grazing the pasture, there is no need for one. The Common Reeves, who have always seen to the day to day management and administration of the Common and the letting of the enclosures, have now also taken on the bailiff's role.

*

The Common Owners make an annual inspection of the Common — a practice begun in the 1970s by Mr. de Bazille Corbin. On the appointed day in June they all climb aboard a tractor trailer fitted out with straw bales as seats, and tour the Common's acres, to inspect any changes that may have been made of a management nature, and to identify any problems that may need to be tackled. These days environmental issues are taken into account — with the Common now designated an environmentally sensitive area, the Owners are able to obtain Government grants for not doing certain things with the Common they might otherwise choose to do.

*

Mention has been made of racing on the Common. The last race meeting to be held there took place on May 2nd, 1957, organised by the Bungay Race Committee. At the time it was not heralded as the last, and so no special meaning was attached to it, but it ended a tradition first begun around 250 years beforehand.

Racing was of course suspended during the second world war, finally resuming again in 1951, but it did not prove as lucrative or as popular as in pre-war years. An idea of the work involved in maintaining and caring for the course and its equipment can be gauged from an invoice sent to the race committee after the war by Mr. R. H. Sprake, auctioneer, valuer and estate agent of Bungay:

To professional charges, 1939-1952: to secretary's time spent on numerous visits to Outney Common arranging for dismantling of jumps and hurdles and storage of same in stands, supervising restoration of ground crossing golf course, dismantling iron hurdles around car park and arranging labour for removal to surround stands, and subsequent removal of hurdles to safety on military occupation. Various inspections and consultations during military requisition and dismantling of enclosures, sundry inspections following complaints of excessive damage or variations in requisition or during erection of military buildings on parts of race course, periodical inspections after damage by gales or wilful destruction and arranging re repairs, carting undamaged materials, flag poles, hurdles and fencing from inside of stands when broken open, to own premises for safety and storing same, various visits with police endeavouring to trace stolen materials and offenders, discussions with salvage officials and arranging supervising removal of iron hurdles and re-erection at cattle roadway on Common.

Discussions with Common Owners on appeals for reduction of rent during emergency from £20 to £1 per annum. Attending before authorities at Beccles making rate appeal, and attendance at Lowestoft on Inspector of Taxes re-assessments, attendances with Norwich Union inspector re revision of insurance. Supervising restoration of course in preparation for proposed renewal of racing in 1951, meeting Common Owners discussing renewal of lease.

Inspection of stands with Bungay Sports Association, discussing sale of stands and during dismantling of same. Clerical work on general correspondence and payments re all during the past 12 years....£126.

The Bungay Sports Association bought one of the grandstands which was on the Common and re-erected it at the Maltings Meadow at Ditchingham when that was opened as a recreation ground. It has been there ever since, although is now reduced in size following a fire in 1987 which badly damaged it.

*

The Common Owners have been well served by their clerks since the first mention of anyone filling that role in 1846. He was Mr. John Taylor. The next to be mentioned is Mr. George Baker, in 1865, and it may well be that it was he who gave way when Mr. Henry Rushmer was appointed agent and clerk in 1883.

Mr. Rushmer served for 32 years, and when he retired in 1915, Mr. Alfred Cocks took over, and held the post for 15 years until ill health forced him to retire in 1930. That was followed by the Sprake era, with Mr. R. H. Sprake taking over and serving for 25 years. When he retired in 1955, Mr. Peter Sprake succeeded him, and was clerk till 1967.

That was the year the present clerk, Mr. Charles Cunningham, took over. So far he has done the job for 29 years, and in 1989 a presentation of cash was made to him on the occasion of his wedding, to buy a wedding present. His period of office included the controversy over the registration of the Common.

*

The Common has always been a popular spot for fishing, and fishing rights are currently leased to the Suffolk Angling Association, whose members include such clubs as the Bungay Cherry Tree Angling Club. There have been some impressive catches from the stretch of the River Waveney around the Common, with pike, bream, roach, dace, chubb and tench among the fish available. One of the best bags ever was caught in 1992 — a record haul of 167lbs of bream caught by Lowestoft angler Malcolm Runacres.

*

Cattle have not been allowed on The Hards for more than 30 years, except in times of flood. In 1988, following a period of heavy rain which again left The Lows under water, the Common Owners fenced off an area of The Hards to accommodate cattle if they should need to be moved to higher ground if that happened again. Spaces were left in the fence to allow the public through, but these were designed so they could be quickly closed when necessary. The emergency area was used for the first time in October, 1993, following prolonged rain which resulted in The Lows being under water for several days.

*

The goings on Outney Common make a healthy profit for their Owners these days. The dividend per going in 1995 was £85 — a total of £25,000 in all. Some of that money is ploughed back into facilities and projects in the town, however. Bungay Town Trust now owns 52 goings — 47 in 1995 which earned it over £4000. It forms only part of the Trust's income, but it contributed to grants it made to a number of projects — including building extensions at the primary, middle and high schools in Bungay. It means the people of Bungay are benefiting in real terms from the profits made from grazing, golf and other aspects of the working of the Common — something that also happens to a lesser extent through Bungay Town Council, which owns two goings.

*

It has already been said that the golf clubhouse is the only permanent building on the Common, apart from the water pumping station. But there are two historic houses which, though on the Norfolk side of the Waveney in Ditchingham, are very much part of the Outney Common scene.

One is Bath House, nestling at the foot of Bath Hills and surely coveted by everyone who walks past and admires it in its idyllic setting. Its date of origin is unknown, but it was built in the late 17th century, and in 1703 was bought by a Mr. King, whose son, John, built a cold bath there and claimed many miraculous cures, as outlined in a previous chapter.

For much of the 18th century it was owned by the Windham family as part of their Earsham estate, but by the 1780s it had become an alehouse, with Robert Hogg the first named innkeeper up to 1798. By 1816 the house had passed to Sir William Windham Dalling, and was occupied by P. L. Powell Esq. It is unlikely to have been an inn during his occupancy. There were a number of tenants in the ensuing years, and the house came into the Rider Haggard family in 1930, when Lady Rider Haggard bought it for her daughter, Lilias, who lived and wrote at Bath House until 1960. Until recently (1994) it was owned by Mr. and Mrs. Alec Douet.

The other house which is just on the Norfolk side of the river is Ditchingham Lodge, owned by Sir Henry and Lady Rider Haggard's grandson, Commander Mark Cheyne, and his wife, Nada. The oldest part of the building is Tudor, with the more imposing Georgian addition being added by John Jenkinson Woodward, a botanist who came to the area in 1770. The original part was the vineyard keeper's lodge — Bath Hills were originally called the Vineyard Hills, because vines were grown on the sheltered south-facing slopes for centuries.

Originally they were said to be grown there in Roman times. When Earl Bigod came over from France with the Norman Conquest in 1066, it is said he planted acres of vines there to provide him with the " home comforts" he was missing from France. Indeed, in medieval times it was said to be called the Earl's Vineyard because of that. Blomefield's *History of Norfolk* refers to an exchange agreement in 1242 in which William de Pirnhow and William de Broome swapped fishing rights on stretches of the Waveney between Wainford Mill and the vineyard — stretches which would have included the river around the Common.

Ditchingham Lodge was also the home of Admiral Sutton and his wife, Charlotte, already referred to earlier in this book. Her ghost is said to haunt the house even today, with sightings of the woman with brilliant dark eyes being claimed as recently as the 1970s.

Admiral Sir Eaton Travers owned the Lodge from around 1830, and it eventually passed into the possession of John Margitson, Lady Haggard's father. It was he who built rifle " butts" at the bottom of Bath Hills for rifle practice for local military volunteers. They would line up on the Common and fire at the targets over the river, and today, that particular spot is still known as Target Hill.

39. The two varieties of blackberry bush on Outney Common – the more common oval-shaped leaved British blackberry on the right and, on the left, the 'American' variety, with its distinctive spear-shaped leaves.

40. Flora and fauna - a moth rests on a purple willowherb, a plant which flourishes on the Common.

Chapter 18
George's Epitaph

I write these last words of the story of my boyhood as I wrote the first, to the sound of Bungay bells chiming over the Common. Through childhood, youth and manhood, and all the troublous ways of a man's life the Lord has kept me, and in his peace, mercy and kindness I abide in my old age.

The last paragraph of George Baldry's book, *The Rabbitskin Cap.*

George Baldry was perhaps the best known character who could be described as "a man of the Common." He lived beside it virtually all his life, and knew it like the back of his hand, through its changing seasons, its changing moods, its beauty, its peace, its controversy.

Every Bungay person has the chance to know it, too, if they choose, through childhood, youth, manhood and old age. For Outney Common is there, enduringly, always, for all of us to enjoy.

Romantically, I suppose, it has always belonged to the people of Bungay. But though in fact it may not be our right, if we use it with care and respect, what has always been seen as part of Bungay's rich heritage will continue to be ours and our successors as a treasured privilege.

Appendix I

Species list — Bungay Common (all areas) - Suffolk Wildlife Trust, 1986

Achillea millefolium — yarrow
Aegopodium podagraria — ground elder
Aethusa cynapium — fool's parsley
Agrostis canina ssp.canina — brown bent
A. capillaris — common bent
A. stolonifera — creeping bent
Aira præcox — early hair-grass
Alisma plantago-aquatica — water plantain
Alliaria petiolata — hedge garlic
Alopecurus geniculatus — marsh foxtail
A. pratensis — meadow foxtail
Amsinckia intermedia — tarweed
Anagallis arvensis — scarlet pimpernel
Angelica sylvestris — wild angelica
Anthoxanthum odoratum — sweet vernal-grass
Anthriscus caucalis — bur chervil
A. sylvestris — cow parsley
Aphanes microcarpa — parsley piert
Apium nodiflorum — fool's watercress
Arabidopsis thaliana — thale cress
Arctium minus — burdock
Arenaria serpyllifolia — thyme-leaved sandwort
Armoracia rusticana — horse radish
Arrhenatherum elatius — false oat-grass
Arum maculatum — cuckoo pint
Atriplex hastata — spear-leaved orache
Bellis perennis — daisy
Betula pendula — silver birch
Bidens cernua — nodding bur-marigold
Bromus diandrus — great brome
B. hordaceous — soft brome
B. x pseudothominii — soft brome
B. sterilis — barren brome

Bryonia dioica — white bryony
Callitriche stagnalis — water starwort
Caltha palustris — kingcup
Calystegia sepium — bellbine
Campanula rotundifolia — harebell
C. trachelium — nettle-leaved bellflower
Capsella bursa-pastoris — shepherd's purse
Cardamine pratensis — lady's smock
Cardaria draba — hoary cress
Carduus nutans — musk thistle
Carex arenaria — sand sedge
C. hirta — hairy sedge
C. nigra — common sedge
C. otrubæ — false fox sedge
C. ovalis — oval sedge
Centaurea nigra — common knapweed
Cerastium holosteoides — common mouse-ear chickweed
C. semidecandrum — little mouse-ear chickweed
Chenopodium album — fat hen
C. bonus-henricus — Good King Henry
C. murale — nettle-leaved goosefoot
Cirsium arvense — creeping thistle
C. palustra — marsh thistle
Cirsium vulgare — spear thistle
Convolvulus arvensis — field bindweed
Cratægus monogyna — hawthorn
Crepis capillaris — smooth hawk's-beard
C. vesicaria — beaked hawk's-beard
Cynosurus cristatus — crested dogstail
Dactylis glomerata — cock's foot
Danthonia decumbens — heath grass
Deschampsia cespitosa — tufted hair-grass
Dryopteris carthusiana — narrow buckler-fern
Eleocharis palustris — common spike-rush
Elodea canadensis — Canadian pondweed
Elymus repens — couch grass
Epilobium adenocaulon — American willowherb
E. angustifolium — rosebay willowherb
E. hirsutum — great willowherb

Appendix I

E. palustra — marsh willowherb
E. tetragonum ssp. lamyi — square stalked willowherb
Equisetum arvense — common horsetail
E. fluviatile — water horsetail
Euphorbia amygdaloides — wood spurge
Festuca rubra — red fescue
F. tenuifolia — fine-leaved sheep's fescue
Filago vulgaris — common cudweed
Filipendula ulmaria — meadowsweet
Fragraria x ananassa — garden strawberry
Fumaria officinalis — fumitory
Galeopsis tetrahit — common hemp nettle
Galium aparine — cleavers
G. palustre — marsh bedstraw
G. saxatile — heath bedstraw
G. verum — lady's bedstraw
Geranium dissectum — cut-leaved cranesbill
G. molle — hedgerow cranesbill
G. pyrenaicum — dove's-foot cranesbill
Glechoma hederacea — ground ivy
Glyceria fluitans — floating sweet-grass
G. maxima — reed sweet-grass
Gnaphalium uliginosum — marsh cudweed
Grœnlandia densa — opposite-leaved pondweed
Heracleum mantegazzianum — giant hogweed
H. sphondylium — hogweed
Hieracium pilosella — mouse-ear hawkweed
Holcus lanatus — Yorkshire fog
H. mollis — creeping soft-grass
Hordeum murinum — wall barley
Hordeum secalinum — meadow barley
Hyacinthoides non scriptus — bluebell
Hydrocotyle vulgaris — marsh pennywort
Hypericum perforatum — perforate St John's wort
H. tetrapterum — square-stemmed St John's wort
Hypochoeris radicata — cat's ear
Inula conyza — Ploughman's spikenard
Jasione montana — sheep's-bit scabious
Juncus articulatus — jointed rush

J. bufonius agg. — toad rush
J. effusus — soft rush
J. inflexus — hard rush
Kœleria maculata — crested hair-grass
Lamium album — white dead-nettle
L. purpureum — red dead-nettle
Lapsana communis — nipple wort
Lathyrus pratensis — meadow vetchling
Leontodon autumnalis — autumnal hawkbit
Linaria vulgaris — toad flax
Lolium perenne — perennial rye-grass
Lotus corniculatus — bird's-foot trefoil
L. uliginosus — greater bird's-foot trefoil
Luzula campestris — hairy woodrush
Lychnis flos-cuculi — ragged robin
Lycopus europœus — gipsy-wort
Malus sylvestris — crab apple
Malva sylvestris — common mallow
Matricaria matricarioides — scented mayweed
Medicago arabica — spotted medick
Mentha aquatica — water mint
M. x verticillata — hybrid mint
Montia perfoliata — buttonhole flower
Mercurialis perennis — Dog's mercury
Myosotis arvensis — field forget-me-not
M. discolor — changing forget-me-not
M. ramosissima — early forget-me-not
M. scorpioides — water forget-me-not
Nardus stricta — mat grass
Nymphœa alba — white water lily
Oenanthe aquatica — fine-leaved water dropwort
O. fistulosa — tubular water dropwort
Ornithopus perpusillus — common bird's foot
Phalaris arundinacea — reed canary grass
Phleum bertolonii — small Timothy
Phragmites communis — common reed
Pinus sylvestris — Scot's pine
Plantago coronopus — buck's horn plantain
P. lanceolata — ribwort plantain

Appendix I

P. major — great plantain
Poa annua — annual meadow-grass
P. bulbosa — bulbous meadow-grass
P. pratensis — smooth meadow-grass
P. subcærulea — spreading meadow-grass
P. trivialis — rough meadow-grass
Polygonum arenastrum — knotgrass
P. aviculare — knotgrass
P. hydropiper — water pepper
P. persicaria — redshank
Potamogeton natans — broad-leaved pondweed
Potentilla anserina — silverweed
Potentilla reptans — creeping cinquefoil
Prunella vulgaris — selfheal
Quercus robur — common oak
Ranunculus acris — meadow buttercup
R. bulbosus — bulbous buttercup
R. flammula — lesser spearwort
R. lingua — greater spearwort
R. peltatus — water crowfoot
R. repens — creeping buttercup
R. sceleratus — celery-leaved buttercup
R. trichophyllus — water crowfoot
Reseda luteola — dyer's weld
Rhinanthus minor — yellow rattle
Rorippa palustris — marsh yellow-cress
Rosa canina — Dog rose
Rubus fruticosus agg. — blackberry
R.lacinatus — cut-leaved blackberry
Rumex acetosa — common sorrel
Rumex acetosella agg. — sheep's sorrel
R.conglomeratus — clustered dock
R. crispus — curled dock
R. hydrolapathum — great water dock
R. obtusifolius — broad-leaved dock
R. pulcher — fiddle dock
Sagina apetala — annual pearlwort
S. procumbens — procumbent pearlwort
Salix sp. — willow

Salvia verbenaca — clary
Sambucus nigra — elder
Scleranthus annuus — annual knawel
Scrophularia auriculata — water figwort
S. nodosa — common figwort
Scutellaria galericulata — skullcap
Senecio jacobæa — common ragwort
S. sylvaticus — heath groundsel
Silene alba — white campion
Sisymbrium officinale — hedge mustard
Solanum dulcamara — woody nightshade
S. nigrum — black nightshade
S. nitidibaccatum — green nightshade
Sonchus asper — prickly sow thistle
S. arvensis — corn sow thistle
Sparganium sp. — bur-reed
Spergularia rubra — red spurrey
Stachys sylvatica — hedge woundwort
Stellaria graminea — lesser stitchwort
S. media — common chickweed
S. pallida — lesser chickweed
Succisa pratensis — devil's-bit scabious
Taraxacum officinale — dandelion
Tragopogon pratensis — goat's-beard
Trifolium arvense — hare's-foot clover
T. dubium — lesser trefoil
T. pratense — red clover
T. repens — white clover
T. striatum — knotted clover
T. subterraneum — burrowing clover
T. suffocatum — suffocated clover
Trisetum flavescens — yellow oat-grass
Tussilago farfara — colt's-foot
Ulex europaeus — gorse
Urtica dioica — nettle
U. urens — annual nettle
Valeriana officinalis — Valerian
Verbascum thapsus — great mullein
Veronica arvensis — wall speedwell

V. beccabunga — brooklime
V. catenata — pink water-speedwell
V. chamædrys — germander speedwell
V. hederifolia — ivy-leaved speedwell
V. persica — common field-speedwell
V. serpyllifolia — thyme-leaved speedwell
V. scutellata — marsh speedwell
Vicia angustifolia — narrow-leaved vetch

Appendix II

A list of those allowed to pasture animals on Outney Common, compiled on April 18th, 1711 by Richard Nelson. Where it mentions "my own" it refers to Nelson.

Market Place: 1 Sir John Playters and Mr. Dalling (now Thomas Miller), 2 Charles Gostling (Three Tuns), now Butcher, 3 William Coats (King's Head, now van Kamp), 4 the same for a decayed tenement, 5 Charles Scales (organist house), 6 John Hemblen senior (Dybal), 7 Titus Tile and George Barfoot, 8 William Brisco (now Bobbit), 9 Robert Aggs (White Swan) and John Botwright (now Knights), 10 Benjamin Debnam and John King, apothecary (now Cockny), 11 William Aldous and J. Gamble (D. Gamble), 12 the same for a decayed tenement, 13 The Cross Keys, late Webster and Smales (now Fleece-Smith), 14 The same, formerly Jey B (?), Cassorne Thomas (?) Stanniet (now Wiseman and John Smith), also two for a decayed tenement.

Great Olland Street (now St Mary's Street): 15 Edmund Hunting (now Rackhams), 16 Peter Mark (now Gill), this house is now...but the commonage I think is Gills, 17 Thomas Southalls (Widow Turner, now William Gambles), 18 Thomas Hill, Maid's Head (now Mathews), 19 Edmund Knights, 20 Robert Youngman (Buck), 21 Matthew Stannard (now Abels), 22 Everard Bass (now Gilson), 23 John King, late Widow Stubbings (Godbole, now Lumby), 24 John Downings, 25 Timothy Hubard (now Smith), 26 Robert Yorke (now Fenn), 27 the same piece of land adjoyning to Mr. Websters and Frestone, 28 Blunderfield, 29 Thomas Hamond (late Hurts), 30 Smiths layte Elmers (Foulger, now Batton), 31 The Meeting House, 32 Edward Hales (now Cole and Kerrison), 33 Richard Nelson, Capitale House, 34 Late Dunets, now Purhills (Batton), 35 Mr. John Dalling (for an ancient tenement where late Holms Barn stands (now widow Sheriffe Kerrison), 36 late Burghill and Mrs. Love (Mr. Wilson), 37 William Rant (now Cudden), 38 William Fisk (now Fristons) (and now Day), 39 Thomas Bunning (now Goodwin), 40 Everard Bass (late Trickers wasted tenement (now Alcock's land), 41 Mr. John Dalling and Mr. Richard Nelson (now Widow Sparl), 42 Frementle of Norwich (suppose next to Widow Sparl).

Olland Street (to Halesworth): 43 Mr. John King (now Mr. Cocking), 44 John Wenn (formerly Shayles, now Mr. Kemp), 45 Andrew Bracy, late Nunns (now John Alcocks), 46 Andrew Bracy stable, late Nunns (now John Alcocks), 47 Samuel Bolton, late Johnsons (now Henry Atkinsons), 48, Everard Bass (late Bidbanks), 49, William Bakers (now Mr. Prentices), 50 Robert Davys Esq. (now Mr. Prentices), 51 Robert Davys Esq. (now Mr.

Prentices), 52 John Jones (late Haspleys, Mr. Prentice), 53 John Jones, the same (Mr. Prentice), 54 Hannah Freeman (my own) and Richard Nelson (late Gowen).

Trinity Street: 55 Mr. James King Capital messuage (now Mr. Jenny), 56 Richard Cooper (now Mr. Ablet), 57 Philip Gosling (now Mrs. Cooper), 58 Charles Scales (late Hemblens, now Moor), 59 late Birking (now Mr. Ablet), 60 Jonathan Bolland, late Gorbold (now Edwards), 61 John Thirkettle, the Black Swan (now Mr. John Hills), 62 Richard Fenn (formerly Skouldings, my own — now Mr. Mapes), 63 Samuel Hemblen, White Lyon (now Richard Harvey).

Bridge Street: 64 John Cunningham 65 Thomas Cole (now Mr. Cunninghams), 66 John Fellingham his wife's right (now Mr. Safford), 67 Mr. Gregory Clarke (now Mr. Williams), 68 Mr. Gregory Clarke (now Mr. Ellis), 69 Thomas Hill (King's Arms, now Mr. Abbage), 70 Mr. Freston (now occupied by Rogby and Alecock), 71 Robert Aggs (now Mr. Plowman), 72 Mr. Gregory Clarke (late Revells — Mr. Robert Moore), 73 Robert Stimpson (now Mr. Botwright), 74 Robert Stimpson (now Mr. van Kamp), 75 late Mr. Frogmorton's, now Mrs. Liffen (Finch), 76 Mr. Bellard (now Mr. Keller).

Back Lane: 77 William Moss, a wasted tenement (now Mr. Winks), 78 Mr. Joshua Nelson (now Mr. Kemps), 79, Widow Spence (now Mr. Ablet), 80 William Young Ye Common Gate (now Mrs. Cooper).

Broad Street: 81 Mr. James King (now Mr. Williams), 82 Mr. Kirke his wife's right (now Mr. Botwrights), 83 Mr. James King, late Nunns (now Mr. Hills), 84 Robert Aggs, his wife's right (now Mr. Botwright), 85 Mr. Joshua Nelson his Capital House (now Mr. Kemp), 86 Mr. Joshua Nelson, a wasted tenement where the Brew House stands (now Mr. Kemp), 87 Mr. Southals (now Mr. Gardiner), 88 Nicholas Shaffton (now Mr. Fox), 89 Mr. Richard Bellard (now Mrs. Nelson), 90 Mr. Richard Bellard (now Mr. Kemps), 91 William Young, formerly Verduns (now Mr. Kemps), 92 William Young, his Capital House (now Widow Pells), 93 Robert Aggs, his wife's right (now Mr. Botwright), 94 Mr. Reeve or Charles Purhill (now Mr. Kemps), 95 William Constance (Mrs. Ayers and Johnson), 96 Titus Tile (now Mrs. Lamb, now Batten), 97 Mr. Richard Bellard (now Mr. Keller), 98 Robert Aggs, late Taylors (now Mr. Plowman), 99 Widow Stebbing (now Cocking), 100 Widow Buxton (now Mr. van Kamp), 101 William Clarke, late Wards (now Clarke as yet), 102 Anthony Brown (now Mr. Barton), 103 Thomas Botwright, the hempland (now Mr. Kemp), 104 Mr. Dalling, late Means (now

Mr. Kemp), 105 John Gage, his wife's right (now Mr. Kemp), 106 Widow Dalling (now Lewis), 107 Mr. James King, late Girlings (now Mr. Negus).

Earsham Street: 108 Mr. Dalling (now Mr. Manning), 109 Mr. Gregory Clarke, late Bacons (now Mr. Prentice), 110, Mr. Gregory Clarke, a wasted tenement, late Tubbys (now Mr. Prentice), 111 Mr. Gregory Clarke, formerly Goss (now Jere. Botwright), 112 Mr. Gregory Clarke, formerly Emits (now Jere. Botwright), 113 Mr. Gregory Clarke, formerly Sayers (now Jere. Botwright), 114 Robert Aggs, formerly Taylors (now Mrs. Botwrights), 115 Popersons tenement (now the workhouse), 116 School House, 117 Widow Lennox (now Thomas Reason), 118 Widow Lennox, 119 The town a wasted tenement occupied per Richard Balls township, 120 Nathaniel Downing tenement, 121 Widow Kingsbury, late Hurts (now Mr. John Kingsbury), 122 Widow Metcalfe and Mr. John Tillney (my own, now Mr. Burt), 123 Charles Asten (now Henry Astin), 124 John House, late Geles (now Andrew Gibbs), 125 William Brierton (now Mr. Salford), 126 William Brierton (Robert Mealam), 127 William Brierton (Mealam), 128 Elizabeth Kirkman (Mapes), 129 Samuel Fuller (Henry Atkinson), 130 Roger Flowers.

Hamblett: 131 Edward Bacon, Bart., 132 Mr. Shephard, 133 Mr. Foster, 134 Samuel Gilbert, 135 Mr. Seaborne, 136 Mr. Richard Nelson, Stow Back, 137 Mr. Richard Bollard, Stockdell Street, 138 Mr. Bays, 139 Mr. Welton (my own), 140 Mr. John Walker, 141 Mrs Metcalfe, 142 Mrs Willson, late Webster, 143 Mr. John Walker, 144 Mr. John Dalling, late Gooch (now Mrs Sheriffe).

*

The Common Owners in 1884, with the number of goings each held:

William Hartcup 34, Sir Edward Kerrison 28, Samuel Smith 26, Mrs Rushmer 12, Mrs. Cooper 10, J. K. Garrod 10, Samuel Smith 22, Henry Smith 12, The Town Reeve of Bungay (Town Trust) 6, Lord Waveney's Trustees 6, G. B. Angel 4, J. H. Smith 1, Samuel Sayer 2, J. H. Smith and Samuel Smith 1, B. Jex 4, James Brandford (executors of Nunn) 4, Henry Alborough 2, Huckbody by Johnson Jethro 4, C. Marston 2, William Tillett 4, Currie Smith and Smith 2, Algar's executors 2, Bedingham and Denton feoffees 2, Henry Rushmer 2, William Bedwell 2, Sarah Algate 4, Trustees of the Independent Chapel, Bungay 2, R. N. Hawkes 2, the Rev Collyer (Vicar of Holy Trinity, Bungay) 2, Mrs. Cracknell 2, H. W. Owles 2, Mrs. Cullingford 2, Miss Walker 2, W. J. Foreman 6, Thomas Grimmer 6, Forster's Trustees 2, Mrs. Savage (trustee) 2, the Rev George Smith 2, Mrs. Legood 8, Francis Chambers' representatives 8, Norman Seeley 4, Miss

Pearce and Stone's executors 4, John Rackham 4, Mark Bedwell 4, J. B. Fountain 4, John Aster 2, George Brown 2, Mrs. Bright 2, J. J. Beaumont 2, Mrs. Jones 2, James Robinson 2, J. M. Robertson 2, Henry Youngs 2, Misses Smith 2.   54 owners in all.

*

The Common Owners in 1968, with the number of goings held :

Manchester Unity of the Independent Order of Oddfellows 43, Brigadier W. G. Carr 23, Miss I. Gower 22, Mr. C. Rogers 20, Mrs. K. Wright 20, Mrs. P. Bowerbank 18, Miss M. J. Day 13, Mr. C. Warnes 10, Mrs. N. V. Owles 10, Bungay Race Committee 10, Mrs. K. Marston 8, Bungay Town Trust 6, Miss E. Whitttrick 6, Mr. Russell Sprake 6, Miss K. Bowerbank 6, Mrs. C. Jordan 6, Miss K. Lawes 5, Mr. Alexander (Miss Sadd executors) 4, Miss F. Pipe 4, Mr. J. Utting 4, Mrs. J. Barrett 4, Mrs. M. Young 4, Mr. H. G. Hadingham 4, the National Trust 4, Mr. E. Newham 4, The Bulls Trust 4, Mrs. Bond 2, Miss A. Rowe 2, Mr. G. G. Sprake 2, Mr. R. R. H. Sprake 2, Mrs. M. J. Clarke 2, Mrs. D. K. Spruce 2, Mrs. D. Watts 2, Mr. P. J. Sprake 2 Bungay Urban District Council 2, Mr. Cannell 2, Bungay Congregational Church 2, Mr. R. Reynolds 2, Mr. J. Gibbs 1, Mr. C. Cunningham 1, Mr. J. A. Sprake 1, Mr. R. Debenham 1, Mr. F. Cornett 1, Buttons Poor Trust 1, Mr. A. G. Sprake 1, the Denton Trust 1: 46 owners in all.

*

The Common Owners in July, 1996, with the number of goings held:

Mr. Roger Duffy 55, Bungay Town Trust 52, Lady Ferrers 23, Mrs. D. Rogers 22, Miss K. Bowerbank 20, Mrs. H. Read 11, Mr. R. Sprake 10, executors of Mr. C. Marston 8, Mrs. M. Youngs 8, The National Trust 6, Bungay Golf Club 6, Mr. B. Frayn-McArdle 6, Mr. J. W. Pipe 5, Mrs. L. D. Pipe 5, executors of Mrs. M. Pipe 5, Mr. B. Fuller 4, Mr. C. Hancy 4, Mr. D. Alexander 4, Mr. C. Barrett 2, Mrs. S. Parker 2, Mr. W. Warnes 2, Mrs. B. Warnes 2, Mr. A. Warnes 2, Miss E. Warnes 2, Mrs. R. Bailey 2, Mr.. C. Cannell 2, Mrs. M. Hancy 2, Emmanuel Church (formerly the Congregational Church) 2, Bungay Town Council (successor to the UDC) 2, Suffolk Wildlife Trust 2, Suffolk Preservation Society 2, Denton Parish Trust 1, Buttons Poor Trust 1, Mrs. A. Cunningham 1, Mr. A. Hancy 1, Mr. D. Debenham 1, Mr. B. Dove 1, Mr. C. Cunningham 1, Dr H. Cane 1, Mrs. A. Sprake 1, Mr. R. Gorbell 1, Mr. R. Hood 1, executors of Mr. W. Harding 1, Mr. W. Mann 1, Mr. G. Mickleburgh 1, Mrs. D. Belcher 1, Mrs. P. Winands-Taylor 1, Mr. D. Sprake 1, Mr. M. Sprake 1, Mrs M. Sprake 1, Nazeland, Ipswich 1:   51 owners in all.

Appendix III

Officers of Outney Common Owners

Outney Common Reeves as at July, 1996: Mrs D. Rogers, Mr. R. Sprake, Mr. B. Fuller, Mr. W. J. Warnes, Mr. D. Alexander, Mr. N. de Bazille Corbin, Mr. A. Hancy.

Outney Common Owners trustees as at July, 1996: Mr. W. J. Warnes, Mr. N. de Bazille Corbin, Miss K. Bowerbank, Mrs H. Read

Chairmen of the Common Owners, with period served: Joseph Parrington, 1865-1883 (?), William Hartcup 1883 (?)-1885, Herbert Hartcup 1885-1914, Austin Smith 1914-1921, Arthur Lawes 1921-1923, Arthur Wright 1923-1956, Nicolas de Bazille Corbin 1956-1984, Mr. Homer Young 1984-1989, Mr. Geoffrey Alexander 1989-1990, Mr. W. John Warnes 1990 to date.

Bibliography

Bungay Common Owners minute books
Bungay Museum archives
Bungay Primary School log book
Bungay Town Trust accounts and minutes
Bungay Urban District Council and Town Council minutes
Duke of Norfolk's Arundel Castle archives
Eastern Counties Newspapers archives
East Anglian Daily Times archives
Suffolk Records Office Archives

Balkeway M G & Derry T K: *The Making of Early & Medieval Britain*
Baldry G: *The Rabbitskin Cap*
Domesday Book, volume I
Dymond D & Martin E: *A Historical Atlas of Suffolk*
Dutt W: *The Waveney Valley in the Stone Age*
Bull J & Edwards B: *A Centenary of Golf on Outney Common*
Ewart Evans G: *The Days That We Have Seen*
Goodwyn E A: *Elegance & Poverty*
Harris J: *The Town Reeves of Bungay*
History Gazetteer and Directory of Suffolk, (White's), 1855
Joby R S: *Waveney Valley Railway*
Mann E: *Old Bungay*
Reeve T: *The Day Bungay Burned*
Reeve T: *Wheel 'em in Bungay!*
Rider Haggard L (ed): *I Walked by Night*
Rider Haggard L: *Norfolk Life*
Room A: *Guide to British Place Names*
Scarfe N: *The Suffolk Landscape*
J B Scott: *An Englishman at Home and Abroad*, 2 vols, 1792-1862